Evita's BOSSIE SIKELELA

Evita's BOSSIE SIKELELA

Evita Bezuidenhout

Design,
Drawings + Dishes –
Linda Vicquery

UMUZI

Foreword

To say I'm a foodie is a *bit* of an understatement ... I have always loved food – particularly South African food. Who doesn't love koeksisters?! I have such vivid memories of my mother cooking kerrieskaapafval with pap en sous, and being outside for a neighbourhood braai. Of my favourite things about South Africa, the incredible food is absolutely near the top of the list. So when I found out that my dear friend and fellow country-lady, Tannie Evita, had a new cookbook coming out, I knew it would give me ample opportunity to enjoy the taste of home.

Evita and I have been friends for years now, a dream of mine having grown up watching that uitgesproke dame on TV. I've been fortunate enough to share the stage with this gem several times, both in South Africa and Los Angeles, and she always knows how to keep me on my toes. With someone full of so many wonderful surprises, I'm sure we can all expect the same from her second cookbook.

CHARLIZE THERON

LEFT: Me and my beautiful friend from Benoni in Hollywood at my presentation there in October 2009

RIGHT: Charlize Theron in Johannesburg with an oom who is her biggest fan

Contents

Tannie Evita's Notes

Unless otherwise stated ...

- all recipes serve 4;
- use medium-sized eggs;
- use full-cream milk;
- use standard level spoon measurements; and
- except when olive oil is indicated, use canola, peanut, sunflower or grapeseed oil.

Conversion table
1 tsp (teaspoon) = 5 ml
1 tbs (tablespoon) = 15 ml
1 cup = 250 ml

Introduction

'After the success of my first cookbook, *Evita's Kossie Sikelela*, there was no way of avoiding the next step: another book focused on what I do best, and that is cooking for reconciliation. Very few people have asked me to explain this, because so many understand that putting people round a table and feeding them with love, can only lead to better things. Imagine how enemies have to change their plans. No fighting round the dinner table; too many knives and forks.

I am proud to be a terminal optimist who is prepared to reinvent the definition of hope. In these dark and dangerous days, my optimism means that I sometimes expect the worst, while hoping that the worst will never be as bad as I imagine. So far, so good. But when I'm in my kitchen preparing a unique and original treat for those I love – and even those I don't even like – my glass is always half full and never half empty. First rule of cooking: pour a lovely glass of wine to be your friend. (Except if you have to drive – then your glass stays empty!)

So from 'kossie' to 'bossie'. I decided to leave the safety of my kitchen for a world tour of South Africa's unique recipes, tastes, foods, feasts and firesides. And so I used whatever time I could muster (running a country does sometimes leave you some Time, especially if it's African!) to travel from the Swartland, via the Klein and Groot Karoo, into the Lowveld, past the Bosveld and towards the Highveld, then across the plains of the Free State, into the glow of Golden Gate to beyond the Garden Route through the Overberg. (Look at the inside of the dust jacket for some impression of my route.)

I hope to expose the tasty, soft underbelly of our rainbow culture in all its diversity. There are different tastes in Paternoster compared to Polokwane, and what is eaten in both is often foreign to those in the Gamtoos Valley. Oudtshoorn is not just famous for ostrich feathers and the Cango Caves, but a perfume of the veld that stays with you forever. So join me in celebrating the culinary art of our multi-talented nation. As you page through this beautiful book, you will go from the San to the suave, from the bush to the baroque, and from the braai-boma to the beautiful beach.

I have added lifesaving tips on various essential treatments and medications I discovered en route during my adventures in veld and vlei. You will find sensible hints on recession-budgeting and allergy-control, even how to make your own salt – the gift of Ocean. Everything made yours with a focus on hope, optimism and my 'yes-we-can' passion. Once again, here is a book full of personal photos of the one they call 'the most famous white woman in South Africa' (if not Africa!), as well as panoramas of our beloved country.

As with the first cookbook, *Evita's BOSSIE Sikelela* is lovingly mentored by my dear friend Linda Vicquery, the expert behind the dishes and illustrations, with a foreword by none other than the pride of our nation, Charlize Theron. Unfolded, the dust jacket is a full-colour poster, backed up by a roadmap of many a delicious culinary journey.'

Setting Off

'If it were not for hope, the heart would break.'
– Thomas Fuller

'I have travelled the length and breadth of our beloved country many, many times and have tasted so many delicious things. Because of my devotion to the art of good cooking, I have always collected recipes on my travels throughout Southern Africa – swopping my bobotie and koeksister recipes while preaching peace and reconciliation. So here are some regional recipes and happy memories of visits to some of my favourite places.'

From Darling...

to De Doorns

'Had I not decided to go via Devon Valley to collect a case of wine from Oom Simmie, maybe I would never have had the pleasure of picking my own waterblommetjies. I spotted a vlei full of these gorgeous flowers – it was September. At first I thought they were water lilies and wanted to take a photograph. Next minute I was up to my knees in water, my designer dress ruined, picking armfuls of these beautiful flowers! When I told Oom Sim, he said that's OK, it was his vlei anyway ...'

"Beulah, peel me a grape!"

'I got the idea of cooking chicken with grapes when I saw Beulah making korrelkonfyt. Living on a beautiful wine farm in the Hex River Valley, she uses vine leaves for so many things – Greek-style dolmades, cheese parcels for the braai, wrapping harders when I bring them fresh from Yzerfontein – in fact, one cannot stop her wrapping anything. These vine-wrapped quail are great for entertaining around the braai.'

Beulah's wrapped quail

Leave hot coals to burn down. Wash and dry the vine leaves. Season the quail and pop a crushed garlic clove in each cavity. Wrap each quail in 2 vine leaves, pressing one over the breast and folding the other underneath. Cover with a rasher of streaky bacon. Wrap each quail in a rectangle of foil, making a well-sealed parcel. Bury the quail parcels in the hot ash, covering well. Leave to cook for 20 minutes, or more if necessary. Remove from the ash, unwrap and arrange on a platter. The vine leaves are delicious to eat as well. Serve with toast made on the braai, spread with crushed garlic, a drizzle of olive oil and a sprinkle of sea salt.

2 vine leaves per quail
1 quail per person
sea salt and pepper
1 crushed garlic clove
  per quail
1 rasher streaky bacon
  per quail

Chicken with grapes

Heat a little oil in a cast-iron pot and brown the chicken. Add the onion and thyme. Season, stir well and sauté for 5 minutes. Add the wine and simmer over low heat for 30 minutes or so, adding water if necessary. Add the grapes and the brandy and simmer for a further 10 minutes, until the chicken is cooked and the grapes are soft. Stir in the crème fraîche and serve immediately with rice.

oil
8 chicken drumsticks
1 small onion, finely
  chopped
1 tsp chopped fresh thyme
salt and pepper
1 cup Late Harvest wine
1 bunch large white
  seedless grapes
1 tbs brandy
2 tbs crème fraîche

Cocktail Hour

Pineapple-chilli

Wet the rims of your glasses. Dip them in a mixture of 1 tbs coarse salt and 1 tsp chilli powder. Fill a cocktail shaker with ice. Add 1 cup tequila, 1 cup pineapple juice and ½ cup fresh lime juice. Shake well and strain into the prepared glasses.

Create your own cocktails – grapefruit, granadilla, pomegranate and fresh lime juice all go well with vodka and tequila.

Lemon & ginger

Squeeze 2 lemons and 5 limes. Bring the juices to a simmer in a pot. Grate a 3 cm piece of fresh ginger and add to the pot. Remove from the heat and allow to infuse for 20 minutes. Strain and pour the liquid into a bottle or jug. Add 1 litre water and 3 tbs sugar. Mix well. Keep in the fridge and add ice cubes just before serving.

Tomato & cucumber

Chop up half a cucumber and mix with 2 peeled and chopped ripe tomatoes in a blender. Add a glass of mineral water, the juice of ½ lemon, a dash of Tabasco sauce and a pinch each of salt and black pepper. Keep it virgin for a non-alcoholic cocktail, or add a tot of vodka to spice things up!

Grapefruit tonic

Infuse a handful of lemon verbena leaves in 2 cups boiling water. Remove the leaves, add 5 tsp sugar and allow to cool. Squeeze 2 ruby-red grapefruit and 2 oranges, and mix the juices with the lemon verbena water. Garnish with strawberries and ice cubes to serve.

Dips for crudité

Egg sauce Combine 2 chopped hardboiled eggs, 1 tsp Dijon mustard, a dash of vinegar and 1 tbs chopped chives with olive oil to make a thickish sauce. Season with salt and pepper. This is delicious with steamed asparagus.

Horseradish dip Combine 1 tbs horseradish sauce, 3 tbs sour cream and 3 tbs plain yoghurt.

Chilli dip Combine 3 tbs plain yoghurt, 1 tbs tomato ketchup and a dash or three of Tabasco sauce.

'How the past just pops out of an old cardboard shoebox! This old photo was taken by friendly Oom Frederik who took a snap of me and my sister Baby among the waterblommetjies. That's what he called us too – 'My ou waterblommetjies!' – before giving us sweets.'

Carole's waterblommetjie chicken

Preheat the oven to 200 °C. Make a béchamel sauce. Add the mushrooms, then the mayonnaise, curry powder and lemon juice. If using canned waterblommetjies, drain and put straight into a greased ovenproof dish. If using fresh, steam them first – they must be firm, not too soft. Cut the chicken into bite-size pieces and add to the waterblommetjies. Pour over the sauce and sprinkle with the grated cheese to cover. Bake for 40 minutes or until the dish is bubbling away and the cheese topping is golden brown. Serve with plain white rice.

2 cups béchamel sauce
120 g mushrooms, diced
100 ml mayonnaise
1 tsp curry powder
juice of 1 lemon
2 x 400 g cans waterblommetjies
  or 600 g fresh, if in season
6 chicken breasts
½ cup grated cheese

Overberg Picnic

'Whenever I travel through the magnificent Overberg I think of Audrey Blignault and her great passion for this beautiful region. A national treasure and always dressed in red, she once did me the great honour of dining with me, complimenting me on my fine cooking. She was the envy of PW Botha, who once said to her: "I wish I had as much influence in the country as you!"

I remember going to see her in Arniston – ons het so lekker gekuier that I stayed on for a few nights. We always soothed ourselves with a cocktail before dinner. We went whale watching, picnicked on the beach, walked through the fynbos and even sat in the middle of a golden wheat field, drinking sangria ... often watched by inquisitive animals, some domestic, but most wild and free.'

Sangria

'This Spanish drink is a deliciously refreshing blend of wine and fruit juice, perfectly suited to our summer climate. You can add chopped peaches or pineapple and more sugar, depending on taste.'

In a large chilled glass jug, combine ⅓ cup brandy, 1 bottle chilled red wine, the juice of 3 oranges, 1 finely sliced orange, the juice of ½ lemon, 1 finely sliced lemon, 2 tbs castor sugar, 3 cups soda water and 2 tbs Cointreau (optional – but I never omit it). Mix well and add 6–8 ice cubes before serving.

Chilli tomato salsa

Roast 5 chillies and 2 ripe tomatoes in a hot cast-iron pan until soft. Peel the burned skin from the tomatoes. Grind the chillies with 1 clove garlic in a mortar. Roughly chop the tomatoes, add to the mortar and pound for a little longer, adding ½ tsp sea salt. Add 2 tbs chopped onion and 2 tbs chopped fresh coriander. Season to taste.

Guacamole

Cut 2 avocados in half. Scoop out the flesh and cut into small cubes. Combine with 1 tbs finely chopped onion, 1 chopped green chilli, 1 large deseeded and chopped tomato and a few sprigs of chopped fresh coriander. Add lemon or lime juice to taste and season with salt and pepper.

Chicken tortillas

'I find tortilla wraps a great hit for picnics, as well as informal lunches or suppers. Always have wheat or corn tortillas in your store cupboard. Experiment with different combinations for fillings, such as chicken, beef, pork, lamb, fish or beans with various salsas.'

Roast 2 chicken thighs, cut the meat off the bone and shred or cut into strips. Mix 3 tbs chopped fresh coriander with 1 small chopped onion and season with a little sea salt. Add the chicken and stir to coat. Place the mixture on one side of a tortilla and roll up. Serve with guacamole and chilli tomato salsa.

Other combinations: sliced pork and chopped pineapple; beef strips with shredded lettuce and green beans; fried fish chunks with chopped spring onions, shredded lettuce and chopped fresh coriander; mince with chopped raw red onion; black-eyed beans and chopped onion; cubed tofu and chopped spring onions.

Wild dagga

'Why not grow wild dagga in your garden? Not only is it beautiful and attracts birds, but it is very useful as a home cure for rheumatism, gout, high blood pressure, painful sunburn and sore muscles.'

Add 3 cups chopped fresh wild dagga to 1 litre water. Bring to the boil in a saucepan, turn down the heat and simmer gently for 30 minutes. Strain and add to your bath.

Night on a Karoo Farm

'Gimme hope, Jo'anna, hope, Jo'anna! I love to play this song driving through the Little Karoo on my way to Johannatjie, my friend on a farm outside Calitzdorp. Her cooking is just irresistible. She's so resourceful and creative, using what is abundant in her veggie garden, like adding grated beetroot to her lamb meatballs and making spicy carrot fritters. She loves cooking outdoors – braaing and stargazing are her two favourite passions. "To think we're made of stardust – anything is possible!" She is well known among her friends as needing 10 minutes to prepare a meal and 2 hours to prepare a feast. She knew I was coming, so a feast it was!'

Onion Stapenade tartlets

'Johannatjie makes her own tapenade, bartering vegetables for olives with friends in Prince Albert. What a wonderful custom – appreciating each others' produce and swapping recipes.'

Preheat the oven to 210 °C. Heat the olive oil in a heavy-bottomed frying pan and sauté the onions and thyme very slowly over low heat, stirring regularly, until translucent. Season well. Roll out the pizza dough and cut into small circles – about 6 cm in diameter or 10 cm for a larger tart. Spread each with tapenade, cover with a spoonful of cooked onion and top with an olive. Place on a baking tray lined with baking paper and bake for 15–20 minutes. Delicious served with chilled white wine or a dry rosé.

2–3 tbs olive oil
4 large onions, finely
   sliced
½ tsp dried thyme
salt and pepper
1 ball pizza dough (p. 86)
¼ cup tapenade
black olives

Tomato confit

Preheat the oven to 180 °C. Halve the tomatoes and remove the seeds. Place the halves on a baking tray and drizzle with balsamic vinegar and olive oil. Season with salt and pepper and sprinkle a pinch of sugar over each. Bake for 20 minutes until soft. Serve as is, as a side dish scattered with fresh basil leaves, or layer with mozzarella cheese and serve as a starter.

12 Roma tomatoes
balsamic vinegar
olive oil
salt and pepper
sugar

Mixed grill kebabs

Soak the kebab sticks in water for 30 minutes beforehand. Remove the skin from the kidneys. Cut in half, devein and clean out the centres. Cut the mushrooms into quarters and remove the stems. To thread the kebabs, alternate the kidney halves, mushroom quarters and bacon chunks, and finish each off with a chipolata. Grill the kebabs over hot coals, turning from time to time, until cooked, or put them under a grill for 10–12 minutes, turning halfway through cooking. Serve with mashed potatoes and tomato confit.

4 wooden kebab sticks
8 lamb kidneys
2 large mushrooms
800 g smoked bacon
4 small chipolatas

Lamb & quince bredie

oil
2 medium onions, finely chopped
3 cm piece fresh ginger, grated
1 tsp ground turmeric
½ tsp red chilli powder
2 tbs chopped fresh parsley
800 g cubed lamb shoulder
quince compote (see below)
salt and pepper
a bunch of fresh parsley

Heat a little oil in a heavy-bottomed pot and sauté the onions until translucent. Stir in the ginger, turmeric and chilli and sauté for a few more minutes, and then add the chopped parsley. Add the meat and a little water and continue cooking over low heat until the meat is tender – about 1 hour. Check regularly as you braise to prevent the bredie from burning. In the meantime, make the quince compote below. When the meat is cooked, add the quince and its liquid, stir gently to combine, season and simmer for a few more minutes. Chop the bunch of fresh parsley and sprinkle over the bredie before serving with basmati rice and a bowl of thick plain yoghurt mixed with freshly chopped chives.

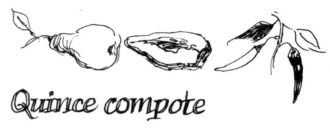

Quince compote

1 cup water
¼ cup sugar
1 tbs wine vinegar
½ tsp red chilli powder
1 quince, peeled, cored and cut into chunks

Make a thin syrup by boiling the water and sugar in a saucepan. Add the vinegar and cook for a few minutes. Add the chilli and quince chunks and simmer for 15 minutes until the quince is soft and just a little liquid is left. For a sambal, dice the quince into smaller pieces.

Johannatjie says: Store quince away from other food. Their strong smell penetrates, so keep in a cool, dry place.

Poached fruit

This is a very easy way of making a quick dessert with fruit of your choice, e.g. 16 plums, or 10 apricots, or 6 large nectarines, 4 pears, or 4 peaches. Rinse fruit well, but don't peel. Halve and depip. Make a syrup in a heavy-bottomed, wide saucepan by slowly bringing to the boil 2 cups water and ½ cup sugar (adjust sugar according to your sweet tooth). When sugar has melted, add the fruit, cover and poach gently until soft, but not mushy – between 5 and 10 minutes, depending on ripeness. Allow to cool and serve at room temperature with cream, ice cream, crème fraîche or mascarpone. Sprinkle with toasted almonds for a special treat.

Plum tart

Preheat the oven to 180 °C. Butter a tart dish and line with the pastry. Prick the bottom with a fork. Halve and depip the plums and pack tightly together, cut side down, in the tart dish. Beat the egg, sugar and cream together and pour over the plums. Bake for 40 minutes or until the pastry is golden. Sprinkle with a little extra sugar.

1 x 400 g roll shortcrust
  pastry
500 g large red plums
1 egg
1 tbs sugar
1 tbs cream

The secret of onions

'You've probably noticed that many recipes begin with "sauté chopped onions slowly in oil until lightly golden ..." The secret of all good cooking (other than Golda Meir's chicken soup) is slow-cooked onions. This is the basis of all good stews, casseroles, sauces and many other dishes. Onions provide sweetness, depth and body, but they must be slow-cooked over low heat and stirred regularly. Never hurry sautéing onions and burn them, or be impatient and undercook them. It will ruin your casseroles. This is the crucial first step to building a dish.'

Onion tart

Preheat the oven to 230 °C and butter an ovenproof tart dish. Press the pastry into the dish and bake blind for 10 minutes. Allow to cool before filling. Turn down the oven to 170 °C. Heat the oil in a frying pan and sauté the onions over low heat until soft and translucent. Remove from the heat and allow to cool. In a bowl, beat together the eggs, milk and cream, then whisk in the flour. Add the cooled onions and mix. Season with nutmeg, salt and pepper. Pour the mixture into the cooled pastry shell and bake for 30–40 minutes, or until the filling is set.

Variation: To this basic tart you can add anchovies, black olives, thyme or diced cooked streaky bacon.

1 x 400 g roll puff pastry
2 tbs oil
2 large onions, sliced
3 eggs
150 ml milk
150 ml fresh cream
1 tbs cake flour
freshly grated nutmeg
salt and pepper

Red onion confit

Heat the oil in a frying pan and sauté the onions over low heat until translucent. Sprinkle over the sugar and let them caramelise for 2 minutes or so, stirring all the time. Add the vinegar, stir and let it evaporate. Add the cassis, red wine, cinnamon and clove. Season to taste and mix well. Cover and cook over very low heat for 20–30 minutes, stirring regularly until no liquid is left. Remove from the heat and cool before spooning into pots to conserve for 2 weeks. This is great served with everyday pâté or a terrine.

2 tbs oil
800 g red onions, finely
   sliced
2 tbs sugar
3 tbs red wine vinegar
2 tbs crème de cassis
1 cup red wine
1 tsp ground cinnamon
1 clove
salt and pepper

IN THE KITCHEN

Tannie's Tips

PUMPKIN
When you tap a pumpkin and it sounds hollow it will keep better than when there's no sound at all.

LEMON JUICE
To get more juice from a lemon or orange roll on a hard surface or press & roll between your hands.

FRITTERS
For a crispy batter don't fry too many fritters at the same time.

FENNEL SALT
Take 1 soupspoon sea salt, 1 soupspoon fennel seeds and crush together in a mortar. Use for fish or chicken before grilling.

CAULIFLOWER
Add a bay leaf to boiling water when cooking cauliflower to prevent smelly odours.

PEELING TOMATOES
Pour boiling water over tomatoes in a bowl. Leave for a minute, then cool under cold tap. The skin now slides off easily.

Carrot terrine

Preheat the oven to 200 °C. Butter a small terrine dish or 15 x 10 cm loaf tin. Heat a little oil in a heavy-bottomed pot and slowly sauté the onion until translucent, adding the ginger, cumin and curry powder and stirring regularly. Add the carrots, salt, sugar and a little water. Stir and add a little more water. Cook the carrots until they are soft and all the moisture has evaporated. Remove from the heat and use a fork to coarsely mash the carrots until you have a thick, rough purée. Season to taste. In a bowl, beat the eggs and then add the semolina and peanuts. Add the carrot mash and mix well. Pour the mixture into the greased dish or tin and press down well. Place in a dish of hot water (bain-marie) in the oven and cook for 40 minutes or until the terrine comes away from the sides. Allow to cool before refrigerating for a few hours. Turn over onto a serving dish and serve cold as a starter with the chilli salsa alongside.

oil
1 medium onion, chopped
3 cm piece fresh ginger, grated
1 tsp ground cumin
1 tsp curry powder
800 g carrots, peeled and diced
½ tsp salt
1 tsp sugar
salt and pepper
2 eggs
1 tbs fine semolina
2 tbs crushed peanuts

Chilli salsa

4 green chillies, chopped
2 cloves garlic, crushed
oil
4 shallots or spring onions, chopped
1 large green tomato, deseeded and diced
1 tbs brown sugar
salt and pepper

Sauté the chillies and garlic in a little oil in a small frying pan. Add the shallots or spring onions, tomato and sugar. Season to taste and cook for about 3 minutes.

Carrot mousse

Cook the carrots as for the carrot terrine above. Mash to make a chunky pâté. Add 1 tsp lemon juice, a few drops of Tabasco sauce and 1–2 tbs smooth plain cottage cheese. Taste and adjust seasoning. Serve on herb toasts or seed biscuits with drinks.

A Good Catch in Plett

'I loved spending time in Plettenberg Bay with the best fisherwoman in the world. (En route to Plett, I usually took a welcome tea break in Hartenbos to see Dalene Matthee who wrote *Kringe in 'n bos*. I was her "Tannie in die bos"!) Whenever I craved really fresh fish – or high adventure – Dulcie took me up the Keurbooms River in her boat. Ja-nee, there was always something exciting happening on that river. We would pack the cool box and off we would go. What a treat seeing flashes of crimson as I sipped a glass of chilled white wine – Knysna loeries flying overhead. And when the fish eagles called, my heart soared. Dulcie would always catch something – my favourite was grunter, caught in the lagoon as the tide turned. Things are different these days. When buying fish, choose those from sustainable sources.'

Grilled grunter

Grunter is so delicious, it's best served with nothing more than lemon wedges. Brush a whole fish with olive oil and sprinkle coarse salt inside the cavity and on the skin. Cook the fish on a baking tray in a preheated 180 °C oven for 20 minutes or so, until the skin bubbles, or on the braai in a fish basket over moderate coals, turning regularly until the skin bubbles and blisters. Do not overcook! For a special treat, serve with lemon butter: melt ½ cup butter with 2 tbs lemon juice, salt and pepper.

Dulcie Says:

Fish bone in throat – dip a little piece of cottonwool in oil and swallow. The fish bone will lodge in the cottonwool.

Baked kabeljou

Preheat the oven to 180 °C. Arrange a whole fish in an ovenproof dish on a bed of sliced leeks, sliced courgettes, black olives, fennel fronds, fresh parsley and garlic cloves. Drizzle over some olive oil and ½ cup dry white wine. Season with salt and pepper. Cook in the oven until baked through. A medium-sized fish should take 20–30 minutes; a big fish (about 3 kg) may take 1 hour. Serve with plain rice to absorb the sauce or boiled baby potatoes. Kabeljou is also delicious grilled on the braai. Scent the coals with dried fennel sticks or dried rosemary twigs.

Fish salad

Flake leftover fish – grunter, kabeljou, kingklip, yellowtail, Cape salmon – and put in a bowl with capers, chopped spring onions, chives and parsley. Mix gently with a vinaigrette (p. 111) or a dressing of olive oil, lemon juice, salt and pepper.

Eat grunter only if you catch it yourself!

The Little Karoo

'I always wear my mohair hat and cardigan when I pass through Prince Albert on my way to De Rust. As I drive along the Swartberg Pass, these are my good luck charms against vertigo so that I don't drive over the edge of this spectacular pass. The Klein Karoo is a magical place with unique industries such as Angora goat, olive and ostrich farms – I buy my feather boas, ostrich steaks and biltong in beautiful Oudtshoorn. Oom Rudolph always invites me to share one of his famous potjies during the Klein Karoo Fees. Dear Pik Botha is quite jealous of him (he needn't be though, as he should know he is my favourite). Rudi also makes meatballs, stir-fries, quick steaks and his very own Outeniqua Rot goulash. He puts so much red wine in his potjie that his guests are known to become more than just philosophical.'

Cheese & olive clafoutis

Preheat the oven to 220 °C and butter a gratin dish. Crush the goat's cheese with a fork. Beat the eggs in a bowl. Add the crème fraîche, milk, nutmeg, thyme and goat's cheese. Mix gently to combine and pour into the prepared dish. Decorate with the olives and bake for 15–20 minutes. The mixture can also be divided into four small gratin dishes or ramekins to serve individually with a green salad.

350 g goat's milk cheese
4 eggs
200 ml crème fraîche
200 ml full-cream milk
2 pinches ground nutmeg
1 tsp dried thyme
200 g pitted black olives

Ostrich in red wine

Sauté the onions in oil in a large cast-iron pot until soft. Add the meat and brown on both sides. Add the carrots, tomatoes, garlic and sugar. Pour in the wine and stock. Cover and simmer for 2–3 hours, or until the meat is tender. Add more wine if necessary. To thicken the sauce, add the semolina towards the end of cooking. Season well and serve with putupap or white rice and green beans.

2 onions, chopped
oil
1 kg ostrich neck
2 large carrots, peeled and
  chopped
1 x 410 g can chopped
  tomatoes
2 cloves garlic, crushed
1 tsp sugar
2 cups red wine, or more if
  needed
2 cups beef stock
2–3 tsp fine semolina
  (optional)
salt and pepper

Summertime Starter!
Basil
Watermelon
Feta cheese
Black olives
Dribble olive oil,
sea salt + pepper

Ostrich fillet steak

Marinate the ostrich steaks in olive oil and soy sauce for 1 hour. Heat a frying pan and seal the oil-coated steaks on both sides. Do not overcook, as ostrich can be tough – keep them pink inside. Remove the steaks from the pan and keep warm. Add the port to the pan, stir and simmer until slightly reduced. Whisk in a knob of butter and season. Pour over the steaks and serve with potato gratin.

Variation: Make a mustard sauce – stir 1 tbs Dijon mustard and ¼ cup crème fraîche into the pan, simmer to heat and pour over the steaks.

1 ostrich fillet, cut into
  4 steaks
olive oil
soy sauce
1 cup port
a knob of butter
salt and pepper

Grilled courgette salad

4 medium courgettes, cut
into long strips 5 mm thick
olive oil
mixed salad leaves
mustard vinaigrette
Parmesan shavings
black olives

'I could fill a whole book with courgette recipes –
from soups to cakes and everything in between.
This is an easy salad to put together at short
notice.'

Drizzle the courgette strips with olive oil and grill on one side
only. Allow to cool and then arrange on a bed of mixed salad
leaves which have been tossed in mustard vinaigrette. Top
with a generous helping of Parmesan shavings and scatter
over black olives.

Variations: These are endless. Use small mozzarella balls,
capers and anchovies, or slices of roasted red pepper and
goat's milk cheese rounds, or ham and cherry tomatoes with
rocket and Pecorino Romano cheese, or crispy bacon with
butterbeans.

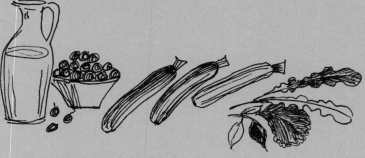

Lamb shanks with lemon preserve & olives

Heat oil in a large cast-iron pot. Add the lamb shanks and brown on all sides. Add the onions and lower the heat. Cook until the onions are translucent, adding a dash of water if necessary. Add the garlic, turmeric, ginger and parsley, stirring to incorporate. Add the lemons and season well. Add the water and stir to combine. Cover and simmer over low heat for 30 minutes, adding more water if necessary. Add the olives and continue cooking for a further 30 minutes until the lamb is tender. Garnish with coriander and serve with creamy putupap, garlicky mashed potatoes or boiled potatoes.

Variation: You can also use lamb shoulder, but cube the meat. To serve, sprinkle over a handful or two of pomegranate seeds and chopped mint.

oil
4 lamb shanks
12 pearl onions, peeled or
    1 onion, chopped
2 cloves garlic, crushed
1 tsp turmeric
1 tsp ground ginger
2 tbs chopped fresh parsley
2 preserved lemons,
    quartered (p. 61)
salt and pepper
1 cup water
1 cup pitted black olives
fresh coriander

Tannie Says:

Keep olives covered with a light brine in the jar once opened. Put a slice of lemon on the surface to stop a mould forming. Mould can be washed away without harming the olives.

Jeebus

'Every now and then I go back to my hometown of Bethlehem in the Free State – just to remind myself of my humble origins. I usually take a detour through the Great Karoo to soak up the vastness of the place and replenish my batteries.'

Pasta shell cake

200g small pasta shells, 2 eggs, 150 ml fresh cream, 50 g grated Parmesan, 50 g toasted pine nuts, salt and pepper, fresh rocket

Preheat the oven to 200 °C and butter a loaf tin well. Cook the pasta shells according to the packet instructions. In the meantime, beat the eggs and cream, add the Parmesan and pine nuts, and season with salt and pepper. Drain the cooked pasta and combine with the egg mixture. Pour into the prepared tin and bake for 30 minutes. Allow to cool before removing from the tin. Decorate with rocket and extra pine nuts and serve at room temperature or cold, with a tomato sauce. This is perfect food for padkos and picnics.

Walnut cake

5 separated eggs, 200 g castor sugar, 2 tsp baking powder, 5 tbs cake flour, 5 tbs cornflour, 1 tbs strong black coffee, 1 cup chopped walnuts

Preheat the oven to 180 °C and butter a round springform cake tin or loaf tin. In a large bowl, cream the egg yolks with the castor sugar until pale and thick. Sift in the dry ingredients, incorporating carefully. Fold in the coffee and walnuts. Whisk the egg whites until very stiff and then fold into the mixture. Pour into the prepared tin and bake for 30–40 minutes. Pierce the centre of the cake with a skewer. If it comes out clean, it is done, otherwise bake for a little longer.

Koffiebus

'What better place to stop for morning coffee or afternoon tea, or to listen to the silence and behold the magnificent view of the famous Teebus and Koffiebus koppies? And with all the talk of flying saucers in the area in the past, maybe I'll do a little UFO spotting.'

Marbled picnic eggs

6 eggs, black China tea, 1 tsp salt, 3 tbs soy sauce, 1 star anise, 1 stick cinnamon

Hard-boil the eggs and drain. Using a spoon, gently tap the eggs until fine cracks appear all over. Put the eggs back into the pot and cover with black tea, adding the salt, soy sauce, star anise and cinnamon. Bring to the boil, then turn down the heat and simmer for 45 minutes. Leave to cool in the liquid. Carefully remove the eggshells. You will enjoy finding the beautiful marble pattern below.

Buttermilk scones

2 cups cake flour, 2 tsp baking powder, 1 tbs castor sugar, a good pinch of salt, 5 tbs butter, 1 large egg, 1 cup buttermilk, a little milk, a little granulated sugar

Preheat the oven to 210 °C and line a baking tray with baking paper. Sift the dry ingredients into a large bowl. Add the butter and rub in with your fingertips. Mix the egg and buttermilk and add to the bowl. Mix well with a wooden spoon to form a dough. Turn out onto a floured surface and knead lightly for a few seconds – not too much. Flatten the dough to 3 cm thick and stamp out scones using a glass or cookie cutter. Place on the lined baking tray. Brush the tops with milk, sprinkle with granulated sugar and bake on the middle shelf for 20 minutes, or until golden.

33

The Orange Farm

'We were always so excited to spend part of our winter holidays with Oom Septie on his citrus farm in the Gamtoos River Valley. What a bon vivant he was! He loved to braai –"kom ons maak hout". Baby and I used to run behind him, collecting kindling on the hillside, while he did the serious wood chopping. Tannie Katie was such a brilliant cook – there was always something comforting bubbling on the wood-burning stove. We loved toast. She toasted slices of homemade bread on the hot plate until they were slightly burnt on both sides. Then the treat of salty farm butter, melting into the warm toast and the pleasure of our first crunchy bite ... that's when we acquired our taste for homemade marmalade.'

Marmalade

'I love the story of how marmalade came to be. About 200 years ago, a Scottish grocer from Dundee bought a shipment of oranges on the cheap. They turned out to be Seville oranges – the bitter kind. What a waste, he thought. But no, his wife had a plan. She cooked them up according to a Portuguese recipe for quince preserve and so created this famous breakfast treat. 'n Boer maak 'n plan! And it is that inventive spirit that has been infused in our people, thanks to the 1820 Settlers.'

Three fruit marmalade

Finely peel the fruit, cut in half and depip. Put the pith of the grapefruit and oranges into a muslin bag. Cut the peel into strips and roughly chop the fruit. If you don't have a preserving pan, put all this into a wide casserole dish. Add the water, bring to the boil and then simmer for about 2 hours until soft. (I sometimes add ½ cup Campari to make a bitter marmalade.) Remove the muslin bag and slowly stir in the sugar until it has dissolved – take your time. Turn up the heat and boil rapidly until setting point is reached. Test after 10 minutes by dropping a spoonful onto a chilled plate, leaving it for a minute. If it wrinkles when pushed with your finger, it will set. Heat a tray of clean jars in a warm oven to sterilise. Let the marmalade cool before ladling into the warm jars. Dear Katie liked to add a tot of whisky to her marmalade before potting.

1 grapefruit
2 oranges
2 lemons
2 litres water
2 kg preserving sugar

Bread & butter pudding

Preheat the oven to 180 °C and butter an ovenproof dish. Butter the bread and spread with marmalade. Arrange in layers in the dish, sprinkling over sultanas as you go. Heat the milk and cream in a small saucepan. Beat the eggs in a bowl and gradually add the castor sugar. Before the milk and cream reach boiling point, pour over the eggs, while continuing to whisk. Pour this mixture over the bread. Bake for 40 minutes until the top has a deep golden crust. Serve warm, with cream or vanilla ice cream.

soft butter
12 x 5 mm-thick slices stale
    French loaf
marmalade
½ cup sultanas
1 cup milk
1 cup fresh cream
3 eggs
75 g castor sugar

'When Oom Septie's friend, Oom Simmie, came to visit, they secretly made mampoer in the farm shed. Simmie also gave Septie his secret recipe for Van Der Hum – ja-nee, 'n volbloed boer, 'n boerejood en die volk – all working together – no wonder our land is so unique. With all those naartjies, Oom Septie made his own version. When Tannie Katie needed cheering up, he would put a tot in her coffee with a dash of cream.

Always full of ideas, Septie used to mix a delicious cocktail for his cousins and friends from the neighbouring farms. I remember them sitting on the stoep at sunset, oohing and aahing. "Septie, wat is in die glas?" They thought they were drinking freshly squeezed orange juice! Mix ⅓ Van Der Hum with ⅔ fresh orange juice in a tall glass, add ice and top with a sprig of fresh mint.'

Marmalade ice cream

I have found a shortcut to serving this delicious dessert. Stir a few spoonfuls of chunky marmalade into soft vanilla ice cream. Mix well. Spoon into dessert bowls, drizzle over some Van Der Hum and sprinkle some toasted chopped almonds on top for a good crunch.

Grilled grapefruit

Cut a grapefruit in half and loosen the segments with a grapefruit knife. Put the grapefruit halves on a baking tray and sprinkle with granulated sugar. Pour 1 tsp Van Der Hum over each half and place under a very hot grill until the sugar caramelises.

Septie Says:

For tummy cramps, rub your stomach with mampoer. For acute cramps, drink strong ginger tea.

Katie's orange duck

Put the duck portions – three pieces at a time – in a large heavy-bottomed pot and render the fat slowly. Remove the duck from the pot and set aside. Add the onions and cook slowly over moderate heat. If there is too much fat in the pot, pour it off – you will only need about 2 tbs to cook the onions. Stir and add the turnips and ginger. When the onions are translucent, add the stock, orange juice, cinnamon and star anise. Season with salt and pepper. Turn up the heat to a bubble and return the duck to the pot. Lower the heat and simmer for about 40 minutes. When the duck is cooked, stir in the marmalade and half of the lemon juice. Season again, taste and add more lemon juice if necessary. Serve with plain white rice.

1 large duck, cut into
  6 portions
2 medium onions, sliced
4 small turnips, quartered
1 stick ginger, grated
2 cups chicken stock
juice of 2 large oranges
1 stick cinnamon
2 star anise
salt and pepper
3 tbs marmalade
juice of 1 lemon

Lemon cake

Preheat the oven to 180 °C and butter a springform cake tin. Cream the butter and sugar until light and creamy. Add the remaining ingredients and mix well. Pour into the tin and bake for 25 minutes. When the cake is cooked, a skewer inserted into the centre will come out clean. To make the syrup, simmer the lemon zest and juice with the sugar and water in a small saucepan for 10 minutes. Once the cake has cooled, remove from the tin and place on a serving plate. Prick the top with a fork and pour over the syrup. Serve warm or cold with pouring cream.

170 g soft butter
170 g sugar
120 g finely ground almonds
50 g almond flakes
1 tsp vanilla essence
2 eggs
zest and juice of 1 lemon
70 g fine semolina
2 tsp baking powder

Syrup
zest and juice of 2 lemons
50 g sugar
2 tbs water

Tannie Says:

An orange face mask is good for oily skin. Squeeze the juice of ½ orange into a bowl. Sprinkle in a few spoonfuls of cake flour and stir until you have a thick paste. Wash your face well before applying the paste with your fingers. Leave on for 30 minutes, before washing off with warm water.

Jannie's Tutti Frutti

'Travelling from Port Elizabeth to East London in the old days, I remember seeing hills covered in spiky plants and little farm stalls along the roadside selling pineapples – Queen Pines! Baby and I would fight in the car until Ouma gave us pineapple sherbet fountains to suck. We loved the acidic-sweet powder that made our palates tingle and kept us quiet. Slim Ouma! I've always loved fresh pineapple juice and nowadays often use it in mixing cocktails. I also use it to tenderise meat. Just drizzle a little on top and leave for an hour or two. Make sure you always have cans of pineapple rings in the store cupboard – they are so useful for quick desserts or Chinese-inspired dishes, like pineapple chicken.'

Pineapple chicken

Mix all the ingredients except the pineapple pieces in a pot. Boil for 3–4 minutes, stirring continuously. Add the pineapple pieces and simmer for 2 minutes. Pour over cooked, sliced chicken pieces or stir-fried chicken breasts. Serve topped with chopped spring onions, on a bed of rice.

2 tbs brown sugar
1 tbs cornflour
1 tbs vinegar
1 tbs soy sauce
1 tsp grated fresh ginger
1 cup fresh pineapple juice, or syrup from the can
1 cup water
1 pineapple, roughly chopped, or 1 x 440 g can pineapple pieces

Frutti kebabs

Soak the skewers in water for 30 minutes beforehand. Combine the pineapple juice, vinegar, honey, salt and pepper. Add the meat and marinate for 1 hour. Parboil the onions for 5 minutes and skin. Cut the red peppers into 4 cm squares. Cut the pineapple into 3 cm cubes. Thread the meat, onions, tomatoes, peppers and pineapple, alternating three times, onto the skewers. Braai or grill the kebabs, basting with the marinade and turning frequently, for about 10 minutes until cooked. Serve with fried rice (p. 41).

4 wooden kebab skewers
½ cup fresh pineapple juice
2 tbs white vinegar
2 tbs honey
1 tsp salt
1 tsp black pepper
1 kg rump steak, cubed
12 pearl onions
2 red peppers
½ pineapple
12 cherry tomatoes

Roasted mangoes

In a bowl, mix the coconut milk, cream and castor sugar. Peel the mangoes and cut into long wedges. Heat the butter in a frying pan, add the mango slices and fry for 5 minutes. Leave to caramelise for a further 5 minutes. Sprinkle with the sugar and leave to caramelise for about 5 minutes, stirring constantly. Transfer the mango slices to a serving plate. Sprinkle with the sesame seeds and serve with coconut cream. Enjoy with a small glass of muscadel.

¼ cup coconut milk
¼ cup thick cream
2 tbs castor sugar
3 large firm mangoes
3 tbs salted butter
2 tbs brown sugar
2 tbs sesame seeds

Fig gratin

Preheat the oven to 180 °C. Wash the figs and cut into quarters without peeling. Place in an ovenproof gratin dish. Cream the egg yolks and sugar in a bowl until pale. Add the cream, whisk together and then add the ground almonds. Mix well and pour over the figs. Bake for about 20 minutes. Serve warm.

16 ripe figs
3 egg yolks
70 g sugar
200 ml pouring cream
60 g finely ground almonds

Cocktail

Combine 1 glass pineapple juice, 1 tbs honey, 1 tsp lemon juice and 1 tot vodka. Top with fresh mint leaves.

Cherry stalk tea

When you depip cherries, keep the stalks and leave them to dry in a warm place before storing in an airtight jar. Place 1 tbs cherry stalks in a teapot and add boiling water to make tea. It's an excellent diuretic!

Spicy cherry soup

'On my biannual visit to Bethlehem, I like to go via Ficksburg to visit old school friends. If it is cherry season, I'm in luck. Tannie Hettie usually gives me kilos to take home, where I like to experiment.'

1 kg black cherries
½ cup water
1 cup red muscadel
1½ tbs sugar
1 stick cinnamon
1 star anise
zest and juice of 1 orange

Wash and depip the cherries. In a pot, bring the water, muscadel, sugar, cinnamon, star anise and orange zest and juice to the boil. Reduce the heat and simmer for 10 minutes. Add the cherries and simmer for a further 2 minutes. Scoop out the cherries and divide among dessert bowls. Pour over the saucy liquid. Serve with vanilla ice cream and crush Amaretti biscuits over the top. Sprinkle with pomegranate seeds when in season (autumn).

Chinese Hot-Pot

'The Chinese are everywhere! Have you noticed those little shops in every town? Missi Hu recommended this hot-pot for easy entertaining. She says food is medicine!'

On a large platter, arrange very thin strips of raw meat – such as fillet steak, lamb, duck, livers, kidney, turkey or chicken. On another platter, arrange raw whole prawns and fish pieces. Put bowls of rice, plain or fried, on the table, as well as a few sauces. Put a fondue pot, electric wok or any other pot suitable for cooking at the table on a little spirit or gas burner. Fill the pot with boiling chicken stock and add a large slice of ginger. Let it simmer over the burner. Your guests serve themselves with rice, and then select a piece of meat. Using a fork, dip the meat in the simmering stock for 1–2 minutes until cooked. Then dip into a sauce. When all the meat has been eaten, add ¼ cup sherry to the stock, along with shredded Chinese cabbage leaves and cellophane noodles. Simmer for a few minutes until tender. Serve this soup in little bowls to end the meal. This is a very convivial way of entertaining. Try it with red wine instead of stock.

fillet steak, lamb, duck,
   livers, kidney, turkey or
   chicken
fish or shellfish, e.g. prawns
plain or fried rice
good-quality chicken stock
ginger
sherry
shredded Chinese cabbage
cellophane noodles

Sauces for Hot-Pot

Soy & ginger
Bring ½ cup soy sauce and 2 tsp finely chopped ginger to the boil. Simmer for 2 minutes.

Plum
Mix 6 tbs plum jam with 1 tbs vinegar, 2 tsp sugar, salt and pepper. Serve cold.

Sweet & sour
Heat 2 tbs vinegar and 2 tbs brown sugar in a small pot until the sugar dissolves. Add 1 tbs cornfour and a dash of fish sauce. Mix. Stir in ½ cup chicken stock and 1 tsp tomato paste. Bring to the boil, stirring continuously, then simmer for 2–3 minutes. Serve warm.

Fried rice

Heat the oil in a large frying pan. Add the beaten eggs and fry until half cooked. Add the rice and stir quickly to coat. Add the ham, spring onions and soy sauce. Fry for 3 minutes, stirring. Turn into a serving dish and scatter over a handful of chopped, toasted almonds.

2 tbs peanut oil
2 eggs, beaten
1½ cups plain rice, cooked
1 slice cooked ham, cut into
   long thin strips
3 spring onions, chopped
1 tbs soy sauce

Evita's Granitas

Watermelon granita

Put 1 kg depipped watermelon chunks in a food processor with 100 g sugar and 1 tbs orange flower water. Mix for 1–2 minutes to obtain a thick purée. Pour the purée into a plastic container and freeze for about 1 hour until crystals form on the surface. Remove from the freezer, stir and spoon into serving glasses. Top with strawberries.

Mango granita

Put the flesh of 2 ripe mangoes into a food processor with the juice of 1 lime. Mix at high speed for 2 minutes. Pour into a plastic container and freeze for 1 hour. Halve 4 granadillas and remove the pulp. Spoon the mango granita into serving glasses and spoon over the granadilla pulp. Decorate with halved slices of lime and fresh mint.

Lemon granita

Bring 2 cups water and 175 g sugar to the boil in a small pot. Reduce the heat and simmer for 20 minutes until the syrup has been reduced by a quarter. Allow to cool. Squeeze 5 lemons and add the juice to the cold syrup. Pour into a plastic container and freeze for 1 hour, stirring from time to time with a fork. Serve in cocktail glasses, decorated with lemon zest and fresh mint.

Mint granita

Chop 50 g fresh mint leaves, reserving 4 whole leaves for decoration. Bring 3 cups water and 160 g sugar to the boil and add the chopped mint. Cover, remove from the heat and leave to infuse for 20 minutes. When cool, filter the infusion. Pour into a plastic container and freeze for 1½ hours. Remove from the freezer and mix with a fork. Put back in the freezer until the granita is firm and crystals have formed. To serve, divide 200 g strawberries between four glasses and cover with the granita. Decorate each with a mint leaf.

Yellow peach mousse

Peel and depip the peaches and cut into small chunks. Purée 4 peaches with the orange and lime or lemon juice. Add the remaining peach chunks and refrigerate. In the meantime, make a coulis. Keep aside 4 raspberries, and place the rest in a saucepan with the castor sugar and water. Bring to a gentle boil and simmer until the fruit has disintegrated. Divide the peach mousse between four glasses and pour coulis over each. Scatter over the pistachio nuts and decorate with a raspberry.

5 yellow peaches
juice of 3 oranges
juice of 1 lime or lemon
300 g raspberries
100 g castor sugar
1 tbs water
20 g pistachio nuts,
  chopped

Campari fruit delight

Place the lemon zest and juice in a bowl. Add the Campari and set aside. Halve and depip the cherries. Peel and depip the peaches and cut into small chunks. Peel the melon and cut into cubes. Halve the strawberries. Add the fruit to the bowl, mix lightly, cover with clingfilm and leave to marinate for 2 hours. To serve, divide the fruit and juice into four large pretty glasses and top up with cold lemonade.

zest and juice of 1 lemon
1 cup Campari
350 g black cherries
4 white or yellow peaches
1 small melon
350 g strawberries
2 cups cold lemonade

Caramelised pineapple

Peel and slice the pineapple. In a bowl, mix half of the butter with the sugar, orange liqueur, and orange zest and juice until creamy. Heat the remaining butter in a wok. Add the pineapple slices and cook for 4 minutes over high heat. Add the orange-butter mixture and allow the pineapple to caramelise slowly. Experiment! Try adding freshly ground black pepper.

1 pineapple
100 g soft butter
50 g sugar
1 tbs orange liqueur
zest and juice of 1 orange
freshly ground black
  pepper (optional)

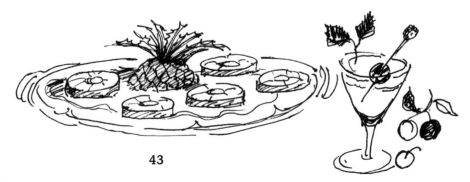

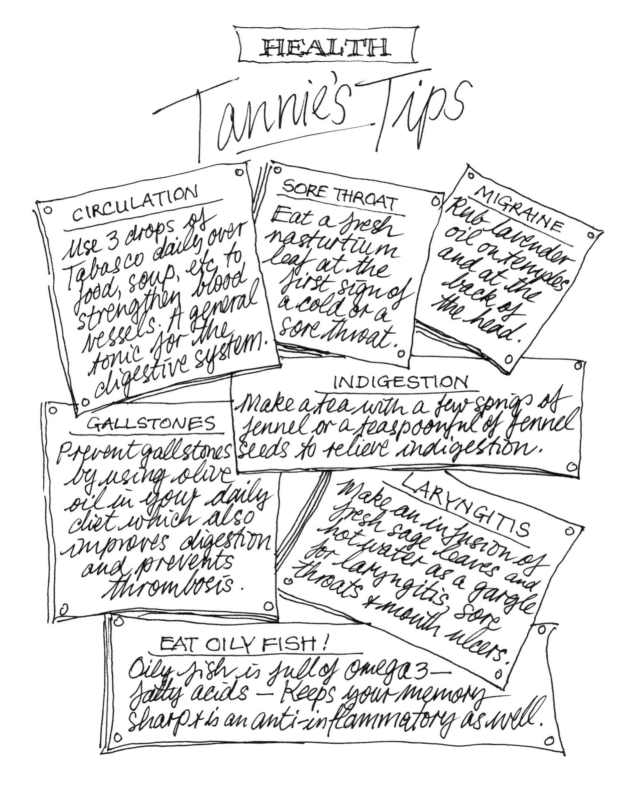

HEALTH

Tannie's Tips

CIRCULATION
Use 3 drops of Tabasco daily over food, soup, etc. to strengthen blood vessels. A general tonic for the digestive system.

SORE THROAT
Eat a fresh nasturtium leaf at the first sign of a cold or a sore throat.

MIGRAINE
Rub lavender oil on temples and at the back of the head.

INDIGESTION
Make a tea with a few sprigs of fennel or a teaspoonful of fennel seeds to relieve indigestion.

GALLSTONES
Prevent gallstones by using olive oil in your daily diet which also improves digestion and prevents thrombosis.

LARYNGITIS
Make an infusion of fresh sage leaves and hot water as a gargle for laryngitis, sore throats + mouth ulcers.

EAT OILY FISH!
Oily fish is full of omega 3 — fatty acids — keeps your memory sharp + is an anti-inflammatory as well.

44

'My grand-
children always
laugh and say that
if I ever audition
for *Idols* and sing
"De la Rey", I must
wear this т-shirt.
Is it because I
look thin?'

Mama Maiti's Morogo

'My heart beats to the rhythm of Africa and when I visit Mama Maiti, I know I cannot possibly live anywhere else in the world. There I find her on her small farm, tending the land; mealies in neat rows in the red soil; spinach, beetroot, tomatoes and green beans, all planted in tune with the moon. You can grow these in boxes on your stoep, she tells me. She has inspired so many people living in towns to plant their own food. Here are some of her ideas.'

Happy marriage – Basil, lettuce, chives, beans

Morogo - wild spinach herbs

'Mama Maiti and the older women in her family collect spinach weeds before she ploughs the land to plant her maize. Isiskwamba can also be gathered after rain on vacant plots or pavements in towns (but not too close to heavy traffic!). These are very nutritious weeds – young shoots of stinging nettle, wild mustard, etc. – but you need someone like Mama Maiti to teach you to identify the good cooking weeds, and you must only pick the young plants. She cooks a good spinach bredie with young beetroot leaves, turnip tops, potato leaves and young shoots of broad beans, peas and pumpkin plants, thus making a small amount of meat go a long way. Johannatjie also does this, never ever scorning a weed in her garden.'

Morogo & potato

Heat a little oil in a pot and sauté the onion until translucent. Add the morogo, potatoes and water. Season with salt and pepper. Bring to the boil and then simmer for about 20 minutes until the potatoes are soft, adding more water if necessary. Add the garlic at the end, cover and leave to stand for a few minutes. I like to drizzle olive oil and squeeze a little lemon juice over my morogo.

oil
1 large onion, chopped
1 large bunch morogo, well rinsed and chopped (about 4 cups)
4 medium potatoes, peeled and diced
1 cup water
salt and pepper
1 clove garlic, chopped
olive oil and lemon juice (optional)

Morogo beef stew

Heat oil in a pot and sauté the onions until translucent. Add the meat and brown all over. Add a little water and braise for 30 minutes. Stir in the morogo and garlic and cook for 5 minutes. Add the tomatoes and simmer over low heat for a further 15 minutes, or until cooked through. Serve with putupap.

oil
2 medium onions, chopped
800 g beef brisket, cubed
1 large bunch morogo, well rinsed and chopped (about 4 cups)
2 cloves garlic, chopped
2 ripe tomatoes, chopped

Planting in tune with the moon

Plant seedlings that produce their seeds or fruit above ground during the waxing phase of the moon.

Plant vegetables that produce crops below ground during the waning phase of the moon – the seven-day period after full moon.

During the last-quarter phase, weed the garden, prune, prepare soil and control pests.

Grow your own medicine – Beetroot!

Plant beetroot in boxes, about 15 cm apart. Grow in light, well-drained soil. Sow during spring, and then thin out. Quick-growing varieties are ready in 2 months. Harvest when they are still small, as they are sweeter.

You can plant vegetables in boxes on the smallest balcony – Swiss chard, green peppers, spring onions, fennel bulbs, sorrel and tomatoes are all suitable container plants.

Chicken & mealie soup

Heat a little olive oil in a large cast-iron pot and sauté the onions and leek until soft. Add the chicken and cook for 10 minutes. Add the corn, stock or water, herbs, garlic, ginger, chilli and orange peel. Season and cover the pot. Bring to the boil and then simmer over low heat for 1–1½ hours, stirring from time to time. Remove the chicken from the bones and return the meat to the pot. Add a little more water if the liquid has reduced too much. Taste and adjust seasoning, adding extra chilli if you like it hot. Sprinkle with mint and serve piping hot with garlic toasts.

Variation: You can use pork or veal instead of chicken and add sweet potato chunks 10 minutes before the end of cooking time.

olive oil
2 medium onions, chopped
1 leek, finely chopped
6 chicken thighs
2 x 410 g cans whole kernel corn, drained
1 litre chicken stock or water
1 tsp dried thyme
2 tbs chopped fresh parsley
4 cloves garlic, crushed
1 tsp grated fresh ginger
¼ tsp chilli powder
5 cm strip orange peel
salt and pepper
chopped fresh mint

Mealie crêpes

Melt 50 g butter in a small saucepan. In a bowl, mix 125 g cake flour and 1 cup milk with a fork or hand whisk. Add 2 beaten eggs, whisking all the time. Add 2 tbs of melted butter, 1 x 225 g can drained whole kernel corn and a pinch of salt. Mix well. Use the remaining butter to cook 4 fairly thick crêpes in a non-stick frying pan. Keep warm and serve with morogo beef stew (p. 47).

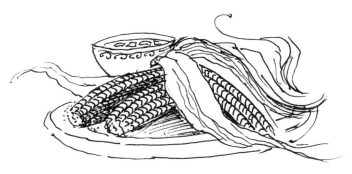

Roasted beetroot

Preheat the oven to 180 °C. Wash and trim the beetroot, reserving the leaves and stems. Boil in a pot of salted water, drain and leave to cool. Rub off the skins. Toss the beetroot in olive oil with the fennel seeds. Place in a roasting dish and sprinkle over the sugar. Roast for about 20 minutes. Meanwhile, shred the beetroot leaves and chop the stems into chunks. Cook in a little salted water for about 5 minutes until tender. Drain and toss with the yoghurt, salt and pepper, and drizzle with olive oil. Serve the roasted beetroot with roast meat or as a snack, with feta cheese and the beet-leaf and yoghurt salad.

10 medium beetroot, with leaves and stems
olive oil
1 tsp fennel seeds
1 tsp brown sugar
2 tbs plain yoghurt
salt and pepper

From the Veggie Garden

'You can easily make the most of a small garden. Train runner beans up a wigwam of bamboo. Sow lettuces from spring to autumn in troughs on your stoep. Rocket grows like a weed, so sow it regularly in a large pot and pick out the leaves for your salads. Chives and most herbs grow easily too – rosemary, thyme, parsley and sage are perfect for window boxes. Nasturtiums are wonderful as you can eat the leaves, flowers and buds. Grow in a pot and let them climb up a trellis if you are short of space. Cherry tomatoes in pots are a treat, as are strawberries. Strawberries in hanging baskets taste good, look beautiful and are full of Vitamin C! You can even grow beetroot, spinach and potatoes in large tubs on your stoep. And don't forget radish – buy 18-day radish seeds for a regular crunch.

Involve your children and grandchildren in helping you in the vegetable garden – growing, weeding, harvesting – to make them aware of nature and organic food. It's an ideal place to learn about the birds and the bees – and it will save your back!'

Cauliflower tabouleh

1 small head cauliflower, 3 tbs olive oil, 2 tbs lemon juice, 2 tbs chopped fresh mint, ¼ cup chopped fresh parsley, 1 clove garlic, chopped, a handful of Rosa tomatoes, diced, 3 spring onions, diced, ½ English cucumber, deseeded and diced, salt and pepper

Grate the cauliflower florets to resemble couscous grains. Mix the olive oil, lemon juice, mint, parsley and garlic. Combine everything in a large bowl, season and mix well. Try this salad using fresh broccoli, different quantities and any other ingredients you like, such as nuts, raisins, bacon and feta.

Mimi's green pepper salad

'Green peppers are not to every-one's liking, but Mimi's creation makes an excellent hors d'oeuvre.'

1 green pepper, 1 tsp finely chopped onion, 3 tbs olive oil, 1 tbs wine vinegar, sea salt and pepper, a pinch of sugar, a squeeze of lemon juice, chopped fresh parsley

Cut the green pepper into thin strips and put in a bowl with the onion, oil and vinegar. Season well and add the sugar, lemon juice and some parsley. Leave to marinate for 1 hour before serving with slabs of feta, hardboiled eggs and good bread.

Veggie appetisers

Mix 2 tbs tapenade with 2 tbs cream cheese and use to stuff tomatoes, cucumbers and celery stalks.

Nasturtiums

Use the whole plant – the flowers are beautiful in salads and vinegar. Use young leaves in a sandwich, as they have a strong pepper flavour, a little like watercress. Flower buds and seeds can be pickled to use like capers.

Nasturtium vinegar

50 nasturtium flowers
3 cups white wine vinegar

Roll the flowers and pop them into a pretty glass bottle. Pour over the vinegar and seal with a screw-top lid. Leave to infuse for 3–5 days. Use a vinegar pourer with a plastic stopper to drizzle over salads, vegetables, etc.

Nasturtium capers

Pick as many nasturtium buds as you can find, from around the end of January. Wash and dry well, and put in a glass jar. Mix 2 cups good-quality wine vinegar, 2 tbs salt and 8 peppercorns and pour over the nasturtium buds. Seal and store for at least 6 months.

Cherry tomatoes

Halve cherry tomatoes and scoop out the seeds. Fill the hollows with egg sauce (p. 14).

The Sardine Run

'People pull up their noses at sardines in our country (they think of them as bait), but I love these beautiful small fish in all their shades of blue – from cobalt and azure to Prussian and periwinkle. Most anglers and sardine lovers look forward to the annual sardine run in winter along the KwaZulu-Natal coast. The kids love catching the twisting, turning fish and bring bucketsful back to the house when we stay with Uncle Jacob and his five wives. There is enough for everyone to eat – including his 22 children. Sardines, being an oily fish, are best eaten fresh and are delicious grilled or braaied. They must be bright-eyed, stiff and arched with steely blue glints. The best accompaniment: lemon wedges, sea salt and a fresh baguette.'

'While visiting our ambassador to Paris, I remember attending a formal dinner at a very expensive restaurant as the guest of President Mitterrand. I sat next to Pierre Cardin – what a dear man. We both ordered grilled sardines and immediately struck up a rapport. The other guests had caviar and lobster (wasting taxpayers' money). Maybe sardines are not chic, but they are honourable, we both agreed, and as he said, if someone does not understand that, it shows they are lacking in intelligence and character.'

Putu-crusted sardines

On a plate, make a dry, spicy mixture of 2 tbs fine mealie meal, a good pinch each of chilli powder and ground cumin, salt and pepper. Gut and clean the sardines, but leave the heads on. Wash under cold running water and slip off the scales with your fingers. Dry with paper towel. Roll the sardines in the spicy putu mixture until well coated. Shallow-fry the fish in hot oil for 3–4 minutes each side or until the crust is golden brown and crisp. Do not allow to burn. Serve with lemon wedges.

Marinated raw sardines

Clean the sardines as above, but remove the heads. Cut through the stomach and flatten out. Remove the backbone. Arrange the fillets on a plate and squeeze over lemon juice, drizzle with olive oil and sprinkle with sea salt. Refrigerate for 1 hour. Try sprinkling a finely chopped shallot over the fillets. These have the superb fresh flavour of the sea and are a great treat for me – better than oysters or caviar! Serve with a glass of chilled white wine.

Stuffed sardines

olive oil
1 onion, finely chopped
2 cloves garlic, crushed
2 tbs chopped fresh parsley
1 bunch spinach, roughly chopped
1 tbs pine nuts
2 tbs breadcrumbs, plus extra to sprinkle
16 sardines

Preheat the oven to 220 °C. Oil an ovenproof dish. Heat olive oil in a saucepan and sauté the onion. Add the garlic, parsley and spinach. Cook over high heat for 1–2 minutes, stirring constantly. Remove from the heat and add the pine nuts and breadcrumbs. Mix well. Clean the sardines. Slit open, remove the head and backbone, but keep the fish intact. Put a spoonful of the stuffing onto the head side and roll up, securing it with a toothpick. Place in the dish, tails in the air and close together. Sprinkle over some extra breadcrumbs, drizzle with olive oil and bake for 15 minutes until the crumbs are golden. These are delicious served hot or cold. For a variation, try adding raisins to your stuffing.

Spanish tortilla

'This Spanish potato omelette is a most satisfying and inexpensive dish.'

olive oil
6 medium potatoes, peeled and cubed
1 onion, chopped
5 large eggs
salt and pepper

Heat a little olive oil in a non-stick frying pan and sauté the potatoes and onion gently over low heat until the potatoes are cooked through. Be careful not to burn them. Remove from the pan with a slotted spoon to drain off the excess oil. Whisk the eggs in a large bowl and add the potato and onion mixture. Season and combine well. Heat 1 tbs olive oil in the pan, pour in the potato and egg mixture and spread out evenly. When browned on the bottom, turn over by putting a plate over the pan and turning it upside-down. Slide the uncooked side back into the pan and cook for a further 3 minutes or so. An easier method is to place the pan under the grill and to cook the top. Cut into small squares to serve as an appetiser or into large wedges for a main course. Serve with homemade tomato sauce or a sweet pepper relish of sautéed onions, red and green peppers, tomatoes and garlic in olive oil.

Variation: Add sautéed red pepper strips to the potato mix or chopped chorizo sausages.

Tapas in Durbs

'Never drink on an empty tummy! Tapas is a great way to start a meal or to enjoy with a drink after work.'

Tapas Ideas
Stuffed tomatoes p.75
Little Kebabs p.75
Meatballs p.59
Chickpea Rissoles p.61

Spicy prawns

Combine the oil, garlic, paprika and sea salt in a bowl. Mix well. Put the prawns in a shallow dish, pour over the marinade and coat well. Leave for 30 minutes or so. Heat a heavy cast-iron pan and add the prawns in batches – don't overcrowd the pan. Cook for 1 minute until the shells turn pink, then turn over and cook for another minute or so. Serve with lemon wedges.

3 tbs olive oil
2 cloves garlic, crushed
½ tsp paprika
sea salt
12–16 large prawns, deveined
lemon wedges

Pan-fried squid (calamari)

Try to find small, fresh squid, otherwise use frozen, but pat dry well before frying. Heat the oil in a heavy-bottomed frying pan. When hot, add the whole squid, tentacles intact, but don't overcrowd the pan. Fry very quickly for 1–2 minutes, then add the garlic, chilli and parsley and toss for a minute to combine. Season and serve immediately with lemon wedges.

12 small squid, cleaned
2 tbs olive oil
2 cloves garlic, chopped
a pinch of chilli powder
1 tbs chopped fresh parsley
salt and pepper
lemon wedges

Potato snacks

Boil small potatoes. Allow to cool before cutting into thick rounds. Mix mayonnaise with capers and spread on the potato rounds. Top with prawns, anchovies, ham, cheese triangles, tuna or anything you fancy. Skewer with toothpicks for serving.

Piperade

Deseed the peppers and chop into small chunks. Sauté the onion and peppers in olive oil over low heat until soft. Add the tomatoes and garlic, stir well, and continue to cook for about 5 minutes. Add the eggs, stirring to combine and cook through. Season and serve on small rounds of toast.

1 large red pepper
1 large yellow pepper
1 onion, chopped
olive oil
2 tomatoes, chopped
2 cloves garlic, chopped
2 eggs, beaten
salt and pepper

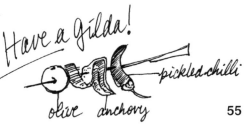

Have a gilda!

pickled chilli

olive   anchovy

55

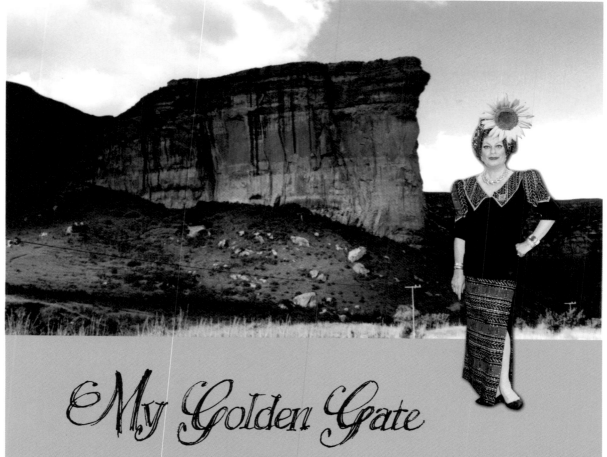

My Golden Gate

'Living in Bethlehem as a child, we used to go to Golden Gate now and again for a weekend treat. Whenever I saw that huge golden fortress of a mountain, it excited me – I saw it as a symbol of hope, as it filled me with joy whenever I went there. It was a gateway through which to escape the humdrum of everyday life in Bethlehem. I loved to watch other campers braaing and I remember being moved by one particular couple. Tannie Dot would run up and down between fire and tent – kaalvoet, cooking potbrood and roosterkoek, wors and chops, mealies and skaapribbetjies. I saw the sublime look of contentment on her husband's face and understood then that the way to a man's heart ... And the peace and quiet that came over the camp at sundown and how happy everyone became – it seemed to hold a key. I was determined to learn the secret and it was then that I realised an essential part of life – to give a good dinner!'

Caramelised pork belly

In a large pot, bring the water and stock cubes to the boil. Plunge the pork belly into the stock, lower the heat and simmer for 1½ hours. In the meantime, mix the honey, soy sauce, vinegar, ketchup and chilli. Season well. Turn off the heat and let the meat cool down in the stock (reserve a few ladles of the stock for the bean purée below). Remove the meat, drain and cut into 3 cm-thick slices. Put the slices into the honey marinade, cover and leave for 2 hours. Braai or grill the pork over moderate heat for about 10 minutes each side, or until lightly caramelised. Pork belly is delicious as a starter snack or main course. Serve hot with bean purée and a green salad.

2 litres water
2 cubes vegetable stock
1 kg pork belly
2 tbs honey
2 tbs soy sauce
2 tbs wine vinegar
2 tbs tomato ketchup
a pinch of chilli powder
salt and pepper

Bean purée

Drain 1 x 410 g can of butter- or red kidney beans. Purée using a hand blender, adding a ladle or two of the reserved stock from the pork belly. Heat in a saucepan over low heat, season well and serve hot.

Beef rib

The rib should be at room temperature before cooking. Drizzle with a little olive oil and soy sauce and leave for 30 minutes. Seal each side for 2 minutes over a hot fire, then braai over medium heat, turning regularly, for about 20 minutes for medium-rare.

   This is even more delicious cooked in a heavy cast-iron pot. Heat 1 tbs olive oil on high heat, add the meat and seal each side for 2 minutes. Add 1 tbs butter, lower the heat to moderate and cook uncovered, turning the meat regularly and basting with the pan juices. Cook for 20 minutes for medium-rare. Leave to rest, covered, for 5 minutes before serving.

1.2 kg beef rib
olive oil
soy sauce
butter

Coconut cookies

Preheat the oven to 150 °C and grease a baking tray. Cream the egg yolks and sugar. Stir in the coconut. Beat the egg white until stiff peaks form and gently fold into the mixture. Place teaspoonsful of the mixture onto the baking tray. Bake for 15 minutes, then reduce the heat to 120 °C and bake for a further 30 minutes until golden brown.

2 large egg yolks
½ cup sugar
125 g desiccated coconut
1 large egg white

The Mystery of Meatballs

'Strange things happen in Bezuidenhouts Valley. I heard this story from Ouma Ossewania. She knew a family who were besotted with meatballs. Two brothers married two Lebanese sisters. The sisters tried outdoing one another to please their husbands and charm their brothers-in-law. Men just love meatballs! When Gert said he preferred his sister-in-law's meatballs, all hell broke loose. Jealousy is a terrible thing. In retaliation, Gert's wife took her husband's favourite hunting rifle and gave it to the Bez Valley Home for Unmarried Mothers to be raffled for funds. Both sisters made superb meatballs and gave Ouma the recipes. "The secret is in the kneading," they both declared.'

'Can you imagine my surprise when, thanks to the sisters, my dear mother introduced me to sumac all those years ago. It is used instead of lemon and can sharpen a dish without making it soggy. Sprinkle over fried foods, fish, salads, rice – anything you like. Put small bowls of sumac on the table for people to help themselves.'

Lebanese meatballs

Pound the mince in a mortar to reduce to a paste or use a food processor to save time. Combine all the ingredients and mix well with your hands. Pinch off pieces and roll into balls. Moisten your palms beforehand, so they don't stick to your hands. Meatballs can be grilled, fried, poached, braised or baked. If you fry them, first dust lightly with flour before frying in oil in a heavy frying pan until brown all over. Drain on paper towel. To poach, bring a pot of good-quality stock to the boil, add the meatballs, cover and simmer over gentle heat for 20 minutes. You can also simmer the meatballs in tomato sauce or yoghurt. For baking, place on a baking tray and bake in a preheated 220 °C oven for 15 minutes. After frying or baking, you can poach them in any sauce you fancy to warm them through. Serve with rice, mashed potatoes, putupap or pasta, or serve with red pepper dip (p. 60) as a snack.

500 g lamb mince
¼ cup fine bulgur wheat
1 medium onion, chopped
1 tsp ground cinnamon
1 tsp ground allspice
a pinch of cayenne pepper
¼ cup chopped fresh
   parsley
salt and pepper

Meatroll surprise

Preheat the oven to 200 °C and oil an ovenproof dish. Work the mince into a smooth paste with your hands. Soak the bread in water, squeeze dry, crumble and mix in with the meat. Add the onion, egg whites, cinnamon, coriander or parsley, salt and pepper. Mix well and knead to a paste. Put the mixture onto a large oiled plate and flatten it with your palms. Put the whole eggs in a row in the centre and fold the mince over them to make a long, fat roll. Pinch the mince firmly at the seam and smooth out the roll so that it will remain intact during cooking. Place the roll in the greased dish and bake for about 20 minutes. Serve with rice and thick tomato sauce. Sometimes the Lebanese sisters would add an extra surprise – soaked pitted prunes next to the eggs. Try it!

1 kg lean beef mince
3 slices stale white bread,
   crusts removed
1 medium onion, finely
   chopped
2 egg whites
1 tsp ground cinnamon
2 tbs chopped fresh
   coriander or parsley
salt and pepper
4 small hardboiled eggs,
   shelled

Red pepper dip

2 medium red peppers, roasted
olive oil
1 small onion, finely chopped
2 tbs dried breadcrumbs
2 tbs crushed peanuts, walnuts or cashews
1 clove garlic, crushed
1 tbs crème fraîche
salt and pepper

Peel and deseed the roasted peppers and dice the flesh. Heat olive oil in a frying pan and sauté the onion until translucent. Add the peppers, breadcrumbs, nuts and garlic and mix well. Pour into a bowl and blend with a hand blender. Add the crème fraîche and season to taste.

Hint: This makes a great pasta sauce. Just add 1–2 tbs pasta water to 2 tbs red pepper dip and pour over cooked spaghetti for a quick supper.

Middle Eastern salad

Place Lebanese meatballs (page 59) on a bed of couscous or bulgur and surround with grilled aubergine. Sprinkle over a handful of chopped spring onion and 1 cup cooked chickpeas. Decorate with chopped fresh mint and toasted pine nuts. Serve with garlic yoghurt.

Preserved lemons

'It is worth making these preserved lemons. Their flavour gives an interesting taste and character to many dishes, including fish dishes, stews, sauces, kebabs and even salads.'

Wash the lemons, dry and cut a deep cross in the top of each. Sprinkle the exposed flesh with fine sea salt then press together again. Place the lemons in a sterilised 1.5 litre-capacity preserving bottle. Add the remaining ingredients and cover with water. Close the lid tightly and leave in a cool area for 3 weeks. Store in the fridge once opened.

10 small lemons
10 tsp fine sea salt
1 stick cinnamon
1 chilli
3 cloves
1 tsp black peppercorns
1 tsp coriander seeds
3 tbs coarse sea salt

Lemon & olive sauce

'The Lebanese sisters gave me this recipe. Serve with fish, chicken or lamb. It's delicious on toast too.'

Rinse the lemon, quarter and remove the flesh. Finely chop the lemon peel. Finely chop the olives. In a bowl, mix the olives, lemon peel, garlic, rosemary or thyme and breadcrumbs. Stir in the olive oil to combine. Add a squeeze of fresh lemon juice and season with black pepper.

1 preserved lemon
1 cup Calamata olives, pitted
1 clove garlic, crushed
1 tsp chopped fresh
    rosemary or thyme
1 tbs dried breadcrumbs
3 tbs olive oil
black pepper

Chickpea rissoles

Blend the chickpeas to a smooth purée in a food processor. Heat oil in a saucepan and sauté the onions until translucent. Add the cumin, garlic and parsley and stir for 1 minute. Transfer to a large bowl and add the chickpea purée, beaten egg and self-raising flour. Season and mix well. Shape tablespoonsful of the mixture into patties using your hands and dust lightly with cake flour. Heat oil in a non-stick frying pan and fry the patties in batches until golden brown on both sides. Drain on paper towel. Serve with olives, chilli tomato salsa (p. 17), fresh rocket and radish, or red pepper dip (p. 60).

1½ cups cooked chickpeas
oil
2 large onions, chopped
1 tbs ground cumin
2 cloves garlic, crushed
3 tbs chopped fresh parsley
1 egg, lightly beaten
3 tbs self-raising flour
salt and pepper
cake flour

Tannie's Tips

PEELING GARLIC
Cut across stem end of garlic. Press down hard on clove with back of big kitchen knife. The skin pops off & the garlic is crushed.

CHOPPING ONIONS
To prevent crying when chopping, put onions in fridge to chill. Put in a bowl of water with ice for 20 minutes to remove bitterness for salads.

CHILLIES
Use dried chillies for slow-cooked stews & casseroles. Use fresh chillies for stir-fries salsas & sambals.

TO PRESERVE
Keep fresh peeled ginger in a small jar of sherry. Preserve fresh chillies in the same way.

CLEANING CHILLIES
Be careful never to touch lips or eyes when deseeding chillies or using cayenne pepper.

SMELLY HANDS
Wash your hands in cold water with a little salt to remove oil & smell after working with garlic or onions.

62

On Cooksisters & Slegte Meisies

❝When I was a little Afrikaans girl growing up in Bethlehem in the old Orange Free State, women who wore make-up were "slegte meisies"– bad girls. My mother was the organist in the local Dutch Reformed Church. She was conservative and strict, in other words, very Afrikaans. We were brought up according to the rules of Church and State. "Don't show off!" "Don't swear!" And above all: "Sies, don't wear make-up!" And: "Meisie? Go back to the kitchen where you are strong!"

I always joke with people who sneer at that idea, knowing they probably don't even know where the kitchen is. "Just follow the cat," I say. But putting together this book has reminded me how grateful I must be for that advice: "Meisie, go and cook! There are no bad girls in a kitchen." How true. There is just no time.

I kept all my secret treasures in a small chocolate box, which I hid in the ceiling of the room I shared with my sister Baby. In it I kept an Easter egg that eventually went white with age. It was the first and last one I ever found in our patch of garden on Easter Sunday. Baby usually ate all the hidden sweets, never sharing with me. I also kept a small black pencil that made smudge marks on my hand. This I would put round my eyes and when I narrowed them and looked in the cracked hand mirror I hid from Mama, I looked like a film star. It was the only alternative to becoming a cook! And so I became a slegte meisie.

In the 1950s I was contracted to Killarney Films in Johannesburg and there it was my job to put on as much make-up as I could. No one there called me a slegte meisie; I was an actress, a real film star. Even my mother forgave me the red lipstick and blue eye-shadow, if I promised to pay all the bills. Mama would sniff: "If it was good enough for Rita Hayworth and Ginger Rogers, it was good enough for my Evangelie Poggenpoel." Me.

"The name has to go!" they demanded when I signed the contract. We eventually decided on Eva Pohl, because it was short and would fit onto the billboards. "Poggenpoel" would end up without the "L"! (And then some naughty boys would add a "P"!) So my first three films changed my life and the way I looked at women wearing make-up. It went further than just lipstick and eye-shadow. Hairstyle was becoming the signature of one's stardom. Looking at pictures of the young Elizabeth Taylor now, you realise that she never changed her hairstyle. Nor has the Queen of England. Consistency, as reflected by Margaret Thatcher's helmet of hair, is realised through careful protection of a look.

Fashion is fickle, like politics. One day it's in, the next day it's out. Your politics becomes the suit you wear, or which handbag and matching gloves you display. It's what you look like, not what you feel. That's politics. But food is without prejudice, it allows pride and you don't have to look your best to be consistent. Barefoot in the kitchen is still my treat.

I still have that small box hidden in my room. In it I keep a photo of me at 12, with black raccoon-lines round my eyes, trying to look like a film star. There is the same cracked hand mirror that reflected my buckteeth and freckles as a teenager. There is the small National Party brooch I wore when my husband became one of Oom Hendrik Verwoerd's ministers. I even have a lipstick I bought in New York at Bloomingdales. I have never worn it in public, because it's too red and will make me look like a slegte vrou. But sometimes when I am cooking and I'm sure no one is around to see, I roll it on and feel 12 years old all over again.❞

63

Fly-fishing in Dullstroom

'Staying with Alice in Dullstroom is always a treat. She has a beautiful trout stream running through her farm and has so many stories to tell. She keeps talking about Truite au Bleu (Blue Trout), which she first tasted as a young debutante living in Paris in the fifties. She loves to recall the flavour, but not the cooking method. Freshly caught trout is killed instantly with a blow to the head, quickly gutted and then plunged into boiling vegetable stock (court-bouillon), which is then turned down to a simmer to cook for about 8 minutes. The trout turns blue and curls up as it cooks. It's delicious with potatoes tossed in parsley butter. You should see Tannie fly-fishing, darlings – there's nothing like freshly caught trout!'

Trout parcels

Preheat the oven to 220 °C. Gut the trout, wipe clean, season the cavities with salt and pepper and stuff with sprigs of fresh dill or fennel fronds. Lay each trout on a piece of foil and sprinkle over a little chopped shallot, a dash of vermouth (such as Cinzano) and a drizzle of olive oil. Cover with lemon slices. Wrap up like a parcel and seal well, but not too tightly. Put in an ovenproof dish and bake for about 20 minutes. Open the parcels and serve immediately – this is a very slimming dinner!

Parsley potatoes

Mix 5 tbs soft butter with ¼ cup chopped fresh parsley. Toss 450 g boiled baby potatoes with the parsley butter while still hot. Season with salt and pepper and a squeeze of lemon juice.

Grilled trout

Gut the trout, leaving the heads on. Sprinkle with salt, put a knob of butter on each and place under a hot grill. Cook until the skin is blistered on both sides. This is my favourite way of preparing trout – don't skimp on the butter.

Fried trout

Dust the trout with seasoned flour. Melt ¼ cup butter and 2 tbs olive oil in a large non-stick frying pan. When sizzling, add the trout to the pan and fry over moderate heat for about 8 minutes until crispy and golden. Turn once halfway through cooking. The flesh should be a lovely, soft, creamy colour.

Alice says:

After fishing all day, her face often gets sunburnt. She soothes it by covering her face with thick Bulgarian yoghurt and leaving it on for an hour or so.

Sophia's ricotta cake

180 g plain chocolate
biscuits
90 g butter, melted
600 g ricotta cheese
1 cup icing sugar
1 tsp vanilla essence
2 tbs Kahlúa
120 g dark chocolate,
grated
2 tbs chopped glacé fruit
½ cup fresh cream

'Sophia Loren's foreword to *Evita's Kossie Sikelela* was the cherry on that koek! And so I am delighted to include her ricotta cake here, which I am sure Helen Suzman (pictured above) would also have enjoyed. All I had in those old days were Marie biscuits. (Blame sanctions!)'

Crush the biscuits and mix with the melted butter. Press into a well-buttered 20 cm springform cake tin with the back of a spoon. Refrigerate while preparing the filling. In a bowl, mix the ricotta, icing sugar, vanilla essence and Kahlúa and whisk until smooth. Add half of the grated chocolate and all the glacé fruit and combine well. Spoon the filling over the biscuit base and refrigerate overnight. To serve, whip the cream until stiff and spread over the cake. Sprinkle over the remaining grated chocolate.

Teatime in Tzaneen

'In Tzaneen I met a man with a sewing machine! Teatime with our beloved friend, Queenie, is an institution. She believes in sharing and communicating through food and that taking tea together in the afternoons is a convivial way of bridging the gap between children and oupas and oumas. Her friends and family bring their favourite treats and everyone shares recipes, advice, news about community projects and, of course, a bit of skinner as well.'

Cinnamon carrot cake

Preheat the oven to 180 °C and grease a large, deep cake tin. In a large mixing bowl, combine the brown sugar and oil and stir in the beaten eggs. Stir in the cinnamon and bicarbonate of soda. Add the flour, baking powder, carrot and walnuts and mix. Pour the batter into the tin and bake for 35–45 minutes, or until a skewer inserted into the centre comes out clean. Cool in the tin for 10 minutes, and then turn out onto a wire rack to cool completely. Combine the cream cheese, vanilla essence and castor sugar well, and smooth over the top of the cooled cake.

1 cup brown sugar
1 cup sunflower oil
3 large eggs, beaten
2 tsp ground cinnamon
1 tsp bicarbonate of soda
1½ cups self-raising flour, sifted
½ tsp baking powder
1½ cups finely grated carrot
1 cup chopped walnuts
1 cup cream cheese
1 tsp vanilla essence
2 tbs castor sugar

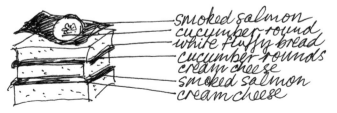

smoked salmon
cucumber round
white fluffy bread
cucumber rounds
cream cheese
smoked salmon
cream cheese

Sandwiches for tea — or drinks!

Children's Birthday Cakes

'My grandchildren are older now and have graduated from decorating baguette rolls with chips and almonds, to helping me ice and decorate more elaborate cakes. If you ask a child what they remember about their last birthday, they are more likely to remember what their birthday cake looked like than the presents they received. And that is what inspires me when I try to make an unforgettable contribution to the birthdays of all the children in my life.'

Requirements

pound cake (or cakes) – number and shape of tin, determined by the cake
icing sugar
food colouring
candles
decoration – sweets, biscuits, etc.
imagination and innovation

Tips

- Adding butter to icing sugar keeps it softer for longer and thus easier to use.
- Most supermarket baking sections have a good selection of edible decorations.
- Add dry food colouring to coconut to obtain different textures, for grass, hair, etc.
- Fill ice-cream cones with sweets and melted chocolate and use as castle towers, clown hats, etc.

Pound cake

250 g butter, at room temperature
250 g castor sugar
1 tsp vanilla essence
4 large eggs, at room temperature
250 g cake flour
1 tsp baking powder

Preheat the oven to 170 °C and grease a 20 x 7 cm loaf tin or a 20 cm round cake tin, depending on the shape of cake you want to bake. In a large mixing bowl, cream the butter, sugar and vanilla essence. Add the eggs, one at a time, beating well after each addition. Sift together the flour and baking powder and gently fold into the butter mixture. Spoon the batter into the baking tin and level out. Bake for 50–55 minutes, or until the cake starts pulling away from the sides of the tin. Leave the cake in the tin for 5 minutes before turning out onto a wire rack.

Bake two loaf cakes for a train cake or two round cakes for a butterfly cake (sandwich them together to make a thick cake). See the drawing. You may find it easier to buy a few large pound cakes and spend the time decorating instead.

68

Butterfly Cake

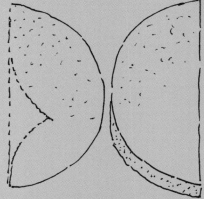

Bake a round cake.
Cut in half, turn
inside out & shape
as indicated.

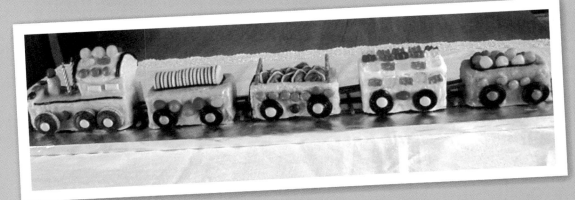

69

Pofadder Pitstop

'On my way to Upington to visit my dear son Izan (he is quite lost now that Oom Eugene is no longer with us, and wants to live near Orania), I stopped over in Pofadder – my goodness me, but it's a hot place! I wanted to visit an old school friend, Magdalena – I call her Maggie. Hasie and her husband used to go hunting together (jy weet mos, die manne hou van saam jag vir die naweek). She's a great cook and gave me her recipes for pofadders and skilpadjies in exchange for bokkoms and korrelkonfyt from the Cape.'

Pofadders

Turn the large intestine inside-out and carefully scrape clean. Cut the heart, liver and kidneys into very small pieces and place in a bowl. Season with salt, and add the pepper, coriander, thyme, Worcestershire sauce and red wine. Stuff the intestine with the mixture. It should resemble a fat snake, slightly greeny-yellow in colour – the pofadder. Don't get a fright – it's delicious. Braai over hot coals.

large intestine, heart, liver and kidneys of a small antelope, such as a springbok
salt
1 tbs black pepper
1 tbs ground coriander
a pinch of dried thyme
1 tbs Worcestershire sauce
1 glass red wine

Hunter's kebabs

'This was Maggie's speciality when the men returned from the hunt with a springbok, but you can also use lamb offal.'

Clean the liver, kidneys and heart by removing the fat and outer membranes from the liver and kidneys and the tubes from the heart. Cut into cubes. Put the meat in a marinade of chopped onion, olive oil, chopped fresh rosemary and lemon juice. Coat well and leave for 1 hour to marinate. Skewer the cubed meat, alternating the kidney, liver and heart twice. Season with salt and pepper and wrap each skewer in a layer of fresh caul. Sprinkle with extra rosemary and braai over medium-hot coals for about 15 minutes, turning and basting with the marinade. The caul melts during cooking and becomes crispy.

Whole liver in caul

'Ask your butcher for some caul. It is the fatty membrane that surrounds a pig or sheep's stomach. Calf's liver is deliciously succulent braaied or grilled whole, wrapped in caul.'

Peel away and discard the outer membrane of a sheep, calf or antelope's liver. Season with salt and pepper and wrap well in a sheet of caul. Brush with oil. Braai or grill on an oiled grid above medium-hot coals for 10 minutes on one side, then turn over and cook for another 10 minutes. Test to see if it is cooked by pressing down on it gently. It should feel firm. Let it rest for a few minutes before carving into thick slices. Sprinkle with a little balsamic vinegar to serve. You can also cut the liver into large chunks and wrap each in a square of caul. Braai over hot coals, turning regularly, for about 15 minutes until done. Season with sea salt and black pepper.

Namibian Fata Morgana

'During my years as ambassadress I once accompanied a trade mission to Morocco and North Africa. The hospitality knew no bounds. I was so excited by the new tastes and flavours that I kept a diary of recipes instead of business contacts. Never mind, I thought, good food is my secret weapon – far more important than securing oil deals ... Many years later, I was invited to cook for President Nujoma. I always insisted on being driven there as I loved the long journey through the verlate vlakte of Namibia. I enjoyed the flaming, dancing heat over the road, and the barren land that looked like shimmering water, causing optical illusions, doubling the landscape and creating great mirages. Ja-nee, I thought, that's just what those politicians do – inflate their own importance. Travelling at a steady speed, I had time to reflect on what I was going to cook for Uncle Sam. He had heard about my famous Reconciliation Bobotie and was dying to taste it, but I had other plans.'

Pomegranate power

'Anything constructed like a pomegranate can only have very special powers. When in season, sprinkle these healthy, beautiful, red gems over casseroles, salads, desserts – in fact, over everything. Or, make this delicious drink.'

Crush the seeds of 1 pomegranate and filter the juice into a tall glass. Add crushed ice, 1 tsp lemon juice and a few fresh mint leaves. Sprinkle a few red seeds over the ice to garnish. Add a dash of vodka for a great sundowner, or ginger ale for a non-alcoholic cocktail.

Chicken in pomegranate sauce

Brown the chicken pieces in oil in a large heavy-bottomed frying pan. Remove the chicken and set aside. Sauté the onion in the same pan, adding more oil if necessary, until golden, stirring regularly. Halve the pomegranates, spoon out the red seeds and discard the pith. Set aside half of the seeds and pound the rest in a mortar to extract the juice. Alternatively, put in a blender for a few seconds to crack the seeds. Strain the juice – you should get about 1 cup. Mix the lemon juice, sugar and water to make a thin syrup. Pour this into the pan and add the pomegranate juice. Simmer and stir. Return the chicken to the pan, season and cook slowly for 1 hour, or until the chicken is tender. Taste and adjust the seasoning. It should have a delicate sweet and sour flavour. Sprinkle over the parsley, almonds and reserved pomegranate seeds. Serve with basmati rice.

4 chicken quarters
 (thighs and drumsticks)
oil
1 medium onion, chopped
4 pomegranates
3 tbs lemon juice
3 tbs sugar
5 tbs water
salt and pepper
1 tbs chopped toasted
 almonds
1 tbs chopped fresh parsley

Caravanserai

'Crossing the Orange River at Vioolsdrift on my way to Grünau, I saw a few haughty camels standing dead still in a sandy kraal near a bustling farm stall. It reminded me of that film *Baghdad Café*. There were caravans parked at odd angles and a few smoky braais going, with a number of colourfully dressed people standing around. It took me back to my travels in the Middle East. I once partook in a heady dinner that lasted all night, as the honoured guest of Sheik Abu Abu el Abu. I'll never forget the exotic dishes cooked over an open fire. I must remember that, I thought at the time – a braai in a caravanserai! And wear something light, cool and flowing. I'm sure if Lawrence of Arabia knew about where we lived, he would have come here as Louwrens van Grünau!'

Kebab Party

'A kebab always reminds me of looking down from the Visitor's Gallery at the opening of Parliament in Cape Town and studying the rows of MPs: white, black, brown, yellow, beige, red, pink, grey, golden – or asleep. Truly kebabbed! What an inspiration for a feast of reconciliation to keep everyone awake!'

Prepare the food in advance and let your guests do the cooking. Standing around the fire makes for a most convivial occasion. Allow for 2–3 skewers per person. Parboil vegetables like baby potatoes, baby beetroot, fennel and pattypans before skewering with the meat. Don't arrange ingredients too closely on the skewer, as everything needs to cook through evenly. And don't pack the kebabs too closely on the grid. Put a selection of sauces and dips on the table and let your guests toast their own bread or putupap over the coals. Below are some ideas for kebabs.

chicken, potatoes, courgettes

Rump, baby beetroot, onion

lamb, red onion, cherry tomato

pork, fennel, pineapple

Pita-askoek

500 g white bread flour, 1 x 10 g pkt instant yeast, 1½ tsp salt, warm water

In a large bowl, mix flour, yeast and salt. Slowly add warm water, just enough to knead into a pliable dough. Leave to rise in a warm spot – about 15 minutes. Pinch off pieces of the dough, then flatten into round discs. Put into hot ash of burnt-down coals. Cover well with ash and leave for 30 minutes or so. Use tongs to remove hot askoek. Test by tapping bread. It should sound hollow. Dust off ash with a tea towel. Dip first into olive oil, then into dukkah or za'atar – a mixture of thyme and salt or sumac. You can also cook askoek in loosely wrapped greased foil. This can be baked directly among moderate coals for about 10–15 minutes.

Stuffed tomatoes

8 large tomatoes, salt and pepper, 150 g couscous, 50 g dried breadcrumbs, 3 cloves garlic, chopped, 5 spring onions, chopped, 3 tbs sultanas, 2 tbs chopped pistachios, 2 tbs chopped fresh mint

Preheat the oven to 180 °C and oil a baking tray. Slice a small circle off the top of each tomato. Using a teaspoon, scoop out the pulp and seeds. Sprinkle salt inside the tomato cavities and turn upside-down to drain. Cook the couscous according to the box instructions. In a bowl, mix the couscous with the breadcrumbs, garlic, spring onions, sultanas, nuts and mint. Season the stuffing and spoon into the tomato cavities. Place on the baking tray, drizzle over some olive oil and bake for 20–25 minutes.

On Safari

Evita goes on Safari

'The Bezuidenhout private game farm just outside Hoedspruit belonged to my dear husband Hasie's family. Being an MP in the NP, he was very well connected. All the leaders of the day spent time there – bosberaad they called it, but I saw what went on! There was one man who visited regularly and who taught me about the Bush, and who stole my heart – dear Pik Botha. Virginia Woolf said: "Nothing has really happened until it has been described – so write many letters and keep a diary." And that is what I did. (Mae West said something similar: "Keep a diary and one day it will keep you." I think that is what Baby, now known as "Bambi", is up to – sies!) So here are some memories, recipes and tips from many safaris with family and friends – and my Romeo.'

Africano cocktail

'Before we set off on safari, I have to give you a recipe of my very own creation – an Africano! Pik was very impressed. We love to sit on the stoep of our rondavel, watching the flaming red African sunset through the thorn trees, sipping this superb cocktail. Between the sunset and the Africano, heaven is on that stoep!'

Mix 1 part brandy with 1 part Van Der Hum. Top up with dry sparkling wine and decorate with a slice of orange.

Variation: Top up with orange juice and it's perfect for brunch.

Beetroot hummus

'This is delicious to serve with drinks and we all know how healthy beetroot is. It is best to use fresh beetroot, roasted, but on safari one has to use provisions.'

Drain the beetroot and mash to make a purée. Add the peanuts, breadcrumbs, cumin, garlic, lemon juice, salt and pepper and mix well to form a thick paste. I use a fork when in the Bush, but you can use a blender at home. Taste and adjust the seasoning, adding more lemon juice, cumin, etc., and add a dash of oil if it is too thick. Garnish with rocket or baby beetroot leaves and serve with toast, seed biscuits or Provitas.

Variation: Use smooth cream cheese or fresh goat's milk cheese instead of the peanuts.

1 x 200 g jar grated beetroot
2 tbs crushed peanuts
1 tbs dried breadcrumbs
1 tsp ground cumin
1 large clove garlic, crushed
1 tbs lemon juice
sea salt and black pepper

Oxtail & onion stew

Lightly dust the oxtail with flour. Warm a little oil in a cast-iron pot and brown the oxtail on all sides. Remove the meat and set aside. Add the onions to the pot and sauté until translucent. Add the oxtail, thyme, wine and sugar. Cover and cook slowly over gentle heat for 2½ hours, checking regularly and adding more liquid if necessary. When the meat falls off the bone, it is cooked. Transfer the meat to a serving dish and pour off as much fat from the pot as you can. Stir in the cream and mustard and turn up the heat. Let it bubble for 5 minutes or so to reduce. Pour the sauce over the oxtail and serve with putupap, rice or potatoes. Pik likes to add leftover boerewors, cut into rounds.

1.5 kg oxtail
cake flour
oil
2 large onions, chopped
3 sprigs fresh thyme
1 cup white wine
a good pinch of sugar
1 cup fresh cream
2 tbs Dijon mustard

Ricotta homemade

1 litre full-cream milk
1 cup heavy cream
½ tsp fine sea salt
juice of 1 lemon

'Whenever I find fresh milk on my travels, I happily make ricotta.'

Combine the milk, cream and salt in a heavy-bottomed pot. Bring to the boil over moderately high heat. Add the lemon juice and continue to boil, stirring constantly and adjusting the heat to prevent overflowing, for about 1 minute until the curds separate. Pour into a strainer lined with two layers of cheesecloth and leave to drain for 1 hour in the fridge over a bowl. Discard the liquid and spoon the ricotta into a container. Cover and refrigerate until needed. This recipe makes 1 cup and will keep for 2–3 days.

Tip: Sprinkle thinly sliced biltong over ricotta and serve on a bed of rocket leaves. For an excellent pasta sauce, add some pasta water to ½ cup ricotta.

'Before I set off for the Bush I make sure that the car is well stocked (sometimes I need a Venter trailer!). I never travel without my Alaskan Uhu chopper – a gift from Sarah Palin! This versatile Eskimo knife can be used for anything from skinning animals to chopping herbs. I take all my favourite provisions – biltong and droëwors, lots of dried and canned pulses like butterbeans, lentils, peas and chickpeas, as well as cans of tomatoes, tuna and sardines – also rice, pearl barley, dried pasta, bulgur wheat, quinoa, pumpkin, butternut, onions, garlic, flour, oil, spices, dried fruit and canned fruit like guavas and peaches, even my very own homemade meringues. One never knows when one may need to make a pavlova! Or who one may have to entertain. I leave it up to Pik to source fresh meat.'

Lentils in red wine with bacon

Bring the lentils, water and red wine to the boil in a pot. Reduce the heat and simmer until tender. In the meantime, fry the bacon in a large frying pan until crispy. Remove the bacon from the pan and set aside. Sauté the onions in the bacon fat with the thyme and garlic, adding a little oil if necessary. Cook until just golden. Return the bacon to the pan. Drain the lentils and add to the pan. Season to taste, mix well and spoon into a serving dish. Lentils are best served warm or at room temperature – and remember, salt is only to be added after cooking the lentils.

Variations: Garnish with 2 quartered hardboiled eggs, or combine the lentils with strips of leftover steak from the braai, or sausages chopped into thick rounds. Toss together in a good, mustardy vinaigrette.

2 cups lentils
1 litre water
1 cup red wine
8 rashers streaky bacon, diced
2 medium red onions, chopped
3 sprigs fresh thyme
2 cloves garlic, crushed
oil
salt and pepper

Butternut & chickpeas

Slowly sauté the onions in oil in a deep casserole dish until translucent. Stir in the garlic, ginger, turmeric, cardamom and chilli and continue cooking over low heat, adding a little water so as not to brown. Add the butternut and stock, bring to the boil and then simmer for 5 minutes. Add the chickpeas and continue to cook until the butternut is tender, but not too soft to fall apart. Add the coconut milk and simmer for 2 minutes. Season, squeeze over the lemon juice, garnish with coriander and serve with basmati rice.

2 medium onions, chopped
oil
3 cloves garlic, chopped
3 cm piece fresh ginger, grated
1 tsp turmeric
5 cardamom pods, crushed
1 small red chilli, chopped
500 g butternut, peeled and diced
1 cup chicken stock
1 x 400 g can chickpeas, drained
1 x 400 ml can coconut milk
salt and pepper
juice of 1 lemon
chopped fresh coriander

Blacks & whites

2 tbs olive oil
1 medium onion, chopped
1 clove garlic, crushed
1 cup lentils
water
1 cup orzo (rice-
shaped pasta)
sea salt and black pepper

'This recipe is part of my reconciliation menu. It is a perfect example of harmonious living.'

Heat the olive oil in a pot over low heat and sauté the onion until pale golden, adding the garlic halfway through cooking. Add the lentils and stir to combine. Add enough water to cover and bring to the boil. Reduce the heat and simmer for about 40 minutes until the lentils are tender and all the liquid has evaporated. Transfer to a serving dish. At the same time, cook the orzo according to the packet instructions. Drain and combine with the lentils. Season to taste and drizzle over extra olive oil if needed. I like to crumble over some feta cheese.

'An essential provision is dried fruit. Being in the heart of the Bushveld in summer, it is impossible to keep fresh fruit. Dried fruit is packed with energy and vitamins, and makes a very healthy snack. I also keep packets in the car as one may come across something fascinating in the veld, which will hold one's attention for hours.'

Dried fruit salad

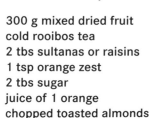

Put the dried fruit in a saucepan and cover with the rooibos tea. Bring to the boil and cook until soft but not falling apart. There should be less than ½ cup liquid left. Add the sultanas or raisins and orange zest. Reduce the heat and stir in the sugar until dissolved and then add the orange juice. Serve warm or at room temperature, topped with almonds and thick Greek-style yoghurt or whipped cream. It's delicious with a splash of brandy or Van Der Hum.

300 g mixed dried fruit
cold rooibos tea
2 tbs sultanas or raisins
1 tsp orange zest
2 tbs sugar
juice of 1 orange
chopped toasted almonds
Greek-style yoghurt or
   whipped cream

Evita's prune mousse

Soak the prunes in the tea overnight in a saucepan. Add the castor sugar and cook slowly until soft. Remove the prunes from the pan and blend with a little of the cooking liquid to make a thick purée. Add the Van Der Hum or brandy. Whip the cream until stiff and fold into the purée. Beat the egg whites to stiff peaks and fold in. Chill in the fridge for a few hours before serving.

300 g pitted prunes
2 cups cold rooibos tea
3 tbs castor sugar
2 tbs Van Der Hum or
   brandy
1 cup whipping cream
2 egg whites

Ouma Elise's health rusks

Preheat the oven to 180 °C. Butter a large, deep baking tin or 2 loaf tins. Combine all the dry ingredients in a large mixing bowl. Beat the eggs and buttermilk and add the melted butter. Add to the dry ingredients and mix to form a dough. Spoon into the tin(s) and bake for 1 hour. Remove from the oven and turn out onto a wire rack to cool. Cut into fingers on a bread board (an electric knife makes this easier to do). Dry out the rusks on a rack in a cool, 100 °C oven for 4 hours, or overnight in the warming drawer.

1 kg self-raising flour
2 tsp salt
2 tsp baking powder
2 cups brown sugar
2 cups rolled oats
3 cups All-Bran Flakes
2 cups sunflower seeds
2 eggs
2 cups buttermilk
500 g butter, melted

Save the Rhino!

'In the Far East, rhino horn is thought to have aphrodisiac powers. Rhino were almost extinct 30 years ago, but thanks to the efforts of South African conservationists their numbers have increased dramatically over the last few years. Unfortunately once more the battle is on. Let us all become involved by supporting those who protect the rhino and encouraging those who catch and punish the criminals who want to destroy them. Gandhi said the greatness of a nation and its moral progress can be judged by the way its animals are treated. Get involved. Visit the International Rhino Foundation at www.rhinos-irf.org.'

'Hasie was always very particular about which kind of wood he was going to use to braai – hardekool of doringboom? He would drive me mad fussing and discussing – indecision is the worst thing in the world. Now you will understand, as do all full-blooded women like me, why I love going on safari with Pik. He knows exactly which wood to use for a potbrood or boerewors – no problem, he just organises the fire and gets on with pouring the drinks.'

Potbrood

In a bowl, combine the flour, salt, castor sugar and yeast. Make a well in the centre and add the oil. Knead, gradually adding the water to make a stiff dough. Knead until the dough is elastic and no longer sticks to your hands. Place in an oiled bowl, cover with a cloth and leave in a warm place until it has doubled in size. Knead again. Place in a well-greased, flat-bottomed cast-iron pot. Grease the lid as well and cover. Place the pot among moderately hot coals, covering the lid as well. Bake for about 1 hour, or until the bread sounds hollow when tapped and a skewer inserted into the centre comes out clean.

6 cups cake flour, sifted
2 tsp salt
2 tsp castor sugar
1 x 10 g pkt instant yeast
7 tbs sunflower oil
1 cup warm water

Stokbrood

The kids love making their own bread rolls. Pinch off pieces of the potbrood dough, roll into long sausage shapes and wrap around sticks. Place on the grid and braai over moderately hot coals for about 20 minutes. Eat these with biltong dip.

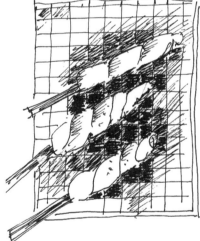

Biltong dip

Mix 1 cup finely grated biltong with ½ cup ricotta or cottage cheese, ¼ cup cream and a generous pinch of black pepper. This also makes a wonderful pasta sauce, diluted with a little of the pasta cooking water.

Hasie's chilli vodka

Hasie's experiment turned out rather well. Decant 1 bottle good-quality vodka into an attractive, clear glass bottle with a tight-fitting cork. Put 4 or 5 small red chillies in the bottle and seal. Refrigerate for 2 weeks before having a tot. Keep in the freezer as vodka is best drunk very cold.

85

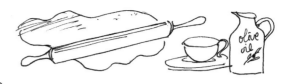

'Being an MP, Hasie did a lot of entertaining. Visitors from all over the world came to the game farm. One group stands out in my mind, as we had so much fun. Two couples – one American and one Italian. The Americans, Johanne and George, are brilliant cooks – they have cooked for their president, just like me, so we understood one another very well. When the Italians, Marco and Rosa, started complaining that they could not face another steak on the braai and were missing the food from their home country, my two American darlings saved the day and came up with this pizza cooked on the braai – genius!'

Pizza dough

15 g dried yeast
a pinch of sugar
1 cup warm water
450 g cake flour
salt
3 tbs olive oil

Dissolve the yeast and sugar in half of the warm water. Sift the flour and salt into a large bowl. When the yeast begins to froth, stir it into the flour with a wooden spoon. Add the oil and enough of the remaining warm water to make a smooth, shiny dough. Knead the dough on a floured board for 10 minutes until smooth and elastic. Add a little more flour if the dough is sticky. Oil a bowl and roll the ball of dough around in it to coat. This prevents a skin forming. Cover the bowl with clingfilm and leave in a warm place for 1–2 hours until the dough has doubled in size. Punch down and knead once more. Divide the dough to make smaller pizzas.

Pizza on the braai

pizza dough
¼ cup olive oil
½ tsp crushed garlic
½ cup grated mozzarella
2 tbs Pecorino Romano, grated
6 tbs canned chopped tomatoes in heavy purée
a pinch of dried origanum

Place the grid about 10 cm above the hot coals. Flatten the pizza dough with your hands on a large oiled baking tray. It is easier to make four small ones. When the fire is hot (you must be able to hold your hand 12 cm above the coals for 3–4 seconds), lift the dough and drape it on the grid. Within a minute, the dough will puff slightly, the underside will stiffen and grill marks will appear. Take care not to burn the underside. Using tongs, flip the crust over onto the coolest part of the grid. Quickly brush the grilled surface of the pizza with olive oil. Scatter over the garlic and cheeses and spoon the tomato sauce over the cheese. Drizzle over 1–2 tbs olive oil and sprinkle over the origanum. Slide the pizza back towards the hot coals, but not directly over them. Using tongs, keep rotating the pizza so that different sections receive high heat. Regularly check the underside to see that it is not burning. The pizza is done when the top is bubbly and the cheese has melted – 6–8 minutes. Try different toppings, but don't cover the entire surface – less is more here!

'After a few days without meat we were wondering how we would manage not having hunting rifles with us. "Leave it to me," said Pik, and off he wandered into the Bush, all alone, without even a drop of water. Two hours later he was back, carrying two guineafowl by their legs, their heads missing. He had spotted them sitting high up in a tree and quietly circled the trunk, keeping his eyes on them all the time. They in turn kept their eyes on him and, as he walked around and around, the guineafowl screwed off their own necks and fell to the ground. Not a shot was fired ...'

Guineafowl with prunes

1 guineafowl
4 rashers streaky bacon, diced
duck fat or oil
1 large onion, chopped
8 cloves garlic, crushed
1 tsp dried thyme
1 bay leaf
2 cups dry red wine
2 cups chicken stock
12 pitted prunes
2 tbs marula jelly

Quarter the guineafowl. In a large cast-iron pot, sauté the bacon pieces in a little duck fat or oil. Add the onion and garlic and cook until soft. Push to the edges of the pot, add the meat and brown. Add the thyme, bay leaf, red wine and stock. Cover and simmer gently over low heat for 2–3 hours until the meat is tender. Add the prunes about 30 minutes before the end of cooking. The liquid should be reduced to about 1 cup. Before serving, stir in the marula jelly. Serve with creamy putupap, boiled potatoes or plain white rice. You choose!

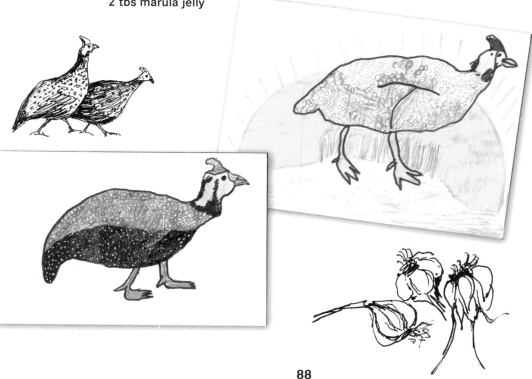

Rosa's sweet & sour warthog

'Rosa introduced me to adding chocolate to sauces cooked with venison, rabbit and meatballs, but try it with turkey and chicken too.'

Make the marinade by mixing all the ingredients together. Marinate the meat overnight or for a minimum of 4 hours. Sauté the bacon in a large cast-iron pot and push to the side. Add the onion and sauté in the fat until soft. Drain the meat and reserve the marinade. Add the meat to the pot and cook for 5 minutes or more to seal. Add the chilli, cinnamon, stock, port and the marinade with its diced vegetables. Cover, bring to the boil and then simmer gently for 2–3 hours, adding water if necessary. In the meantime, make the sweet and sour sauce in a small heavy-bottomed saucepan. Dissolve the sugar in the water, add the vinegar and simmer. While it's simmering, stir in the chocolate to make a smooth sauce. Near the end of cooking, stir the sultanas and peanuts into the stew. Pour in the sweet and sour sauce and combine gently. The stew will have more taste if cooked the day before to allow the flavours to mingle and mellow. Serve with creamy putupap, rice or mashed potatoes.

Variation: Double the quantity of the sweet and sour sauce for a more tangy stew and add lemon juice to taste at the end.

800 g warthog shoulder, cut into small chunks
4 rashers streaky bacon, diced
1 large onion, chopped
½ tsp chilli powder
1 tsp ground cinnamon
2 cups beef stock
1 glass port
2 tbs sultanas
2 tbs chopped peanuts

Marinade
2 cups red wine
2 medium onions, chopped
1 medium carrot, peeled and diced
2 bay leaves
1 tsp dried thyme
3 cloves
1 stick cinnamon
orange zest
1 tsp sugar
salt and pepper

Sweet & sour sauce
3 tbs sugar
½ cup water
3 tbs red wine vinegar
2 tbs grated dark chocolate

Venison ragoût

For a delicious ragoût, follow the recipe for Rosa's warthog, but use any venison you like, cut into very small cubes. After marinating, combine with the bacon and onions, and sauté until soft. Add the marinade and beef stock to the pot and simmer for 2–3 hours until the meat is tender. It becomes very saucy and is delicious spooned over creamy putupap or braaied or grilled putupap squares. Instead of adding sweet and sour sauce at the end, you can add Johannatjie's chilli quince compote (p. 20) and a glass of port. Experiment!

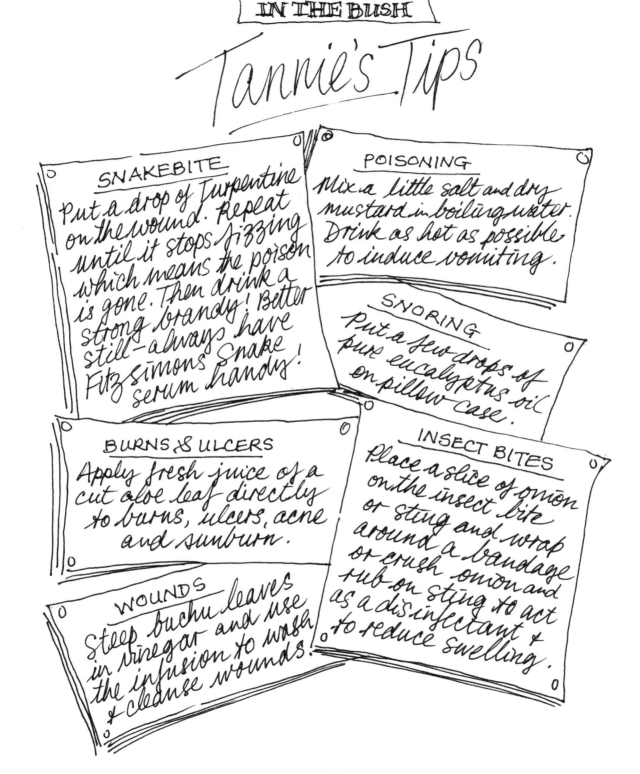

IN THE BUSH

Tannie's Tips

SNAKEBITE

Put a drop of Turpentine on the wound. Repeat until it stops fizzing which means the poison is gone. Then drink a strong brandy! Better still—always have Fitzsimons Snake serum handy!

POISONING

Mix a little salt and dry mustard in boiling water. Drink as hot as possible to induce vomiting.

SNORING

Put a few drops of pure eucalyptus oil on pillow case.

BURNS & ULCERS

Apply fresh juice of a cut aloe leaf directly to burns, ulcers, acne and sunburn.

INSECT BITES

Place a slice of onion on the insect bite or sting and wrap around a bandage or crush onion and rub on sting to act as a disinfectant + to reduce swelling.

WOUNDS

Steep buchu leaves in vinegar and use the infusion to wash + cleanse wounds.

'Pik Botha takes
me hunting in the bush
(no animal was injured or killed
in the process)!'

'Now I am in love with the trees of the Bushveld – without them, the great diversity of birds, animals and insects could not exist. The beautiful baobab with its mysterious flower that opens overnight and is pollinated by bats; the marula, which has so many uses apart from that wonderful drink; the pod mahogany used in traditional medicine – the kids collect the pods and use them as little platters to serve peanuts at cocktail time and also acacia thorns to use as toothpicks! Other trees I love are the weeping boerboon, appleleaf, coral, fever and sausage trees – and many more. I have been studying trees and their uses for years. We should teach our children about the sustainable use of plants and trees. When out on safari with the kids, I encourage them to draw, keep notes and collect interesting things for our nature table when we return to camp. Mof is so good with them, encouraging them to make their own greeting cards using feathers, dried leaves and seeds.'

Nature Table

Nature's Remedies

The baobab tree's fruit is rich in Vitamin C and calcium. The dry fruit pulp can be eaten raw, or mixed with milk, or as a porridge. Leaves can also be used as a tasty soup vegetable. The bark of the sjambok pod tree is used to treat abscesses and skin disorders, while juice from the roots is a cure for bilharzia. An extract of the roots of the russet bushwillow is used to treat stomach ailments. Various decoctions of the buffalo thorn tree are used to treat skin problems and dysentery.

The fruit pulp of the marula is very rich in Vitamin C, while the bark is used to treat diarrhoea. The bark of the pod mahogany can be used to treat eczema. The crushed roots of the white seringa relieves toothache. The sticky resin of the wild teak is used to treat ringworm, blood disorders and skin sores. To relieve colds, rural people burn roots of the appleleaf tree and inhale the smoke. Various preparations of the jackal berry tree are made to treat coughs, dysentery and skin disorders.

Mementoes

'DeKock and Mof love entertaining. They give extravagant dinner parties and then, the morning after – ja-nee. DeKock has a foolproof cure for hangovers, as well as homebrew grog, a very effective anti-flu potion. While he recovers, Mof is full of ideas. He collects wine corks from memorable meals, frames them and gives them away as presents – te dierbaar, my skoonseun. Mof never stops foraging – he even salvages things from rubbish dumps. He picked up some wooden pallets outside a building site once and turned them into spice and plate racks. Recycle, restore, don't waste – he's such a good influence on the kids. Being a creative cook as well, he came up with this Maandag tert and vegetable cake made from Sunday lunch leftovers.'

DeKock's regmaker

Combine 2 tbs brandy, 1 tbs lemon juice, 1 tsp grated ginger and 1 tbs honey in a tall glass. Top up with rooibos tea and a slice of lemon.

Grog

This is DeKock's special anti-flu potion. Mix 1 cup hot water, 2 tbs lemon juice, 1 stick cinnamon and 3 cloves crushed garlic. Drink several times per day.

Monday tart

Preheat the oven to 210 °C and butter a baking tray. Mix the rice with the butter, parsley and origanum. Roll out the pastry into a rectangle. Layer half the rice on one side of the pastry, cover with half the egg slices, season and then lay strips of chicken or meat over the egg. Season again and top with the remaining eggs slices, followed by the rest of the rice. Fold over the empty half of the pastry and pinch the edges to seal. Brush with the beaten egg and place on the baking tray. Prick the pastry here and there with a fork and bake for 30 minutes until golden brown.

Variations: Use leftover flaked fish, chopped vegetables, canned tuna, peas, leeks or quail eggs.

1 cup leftover cooked rice
75 g butter, melted
¼ cup chopped fresh parsley
a good pinch of dried origanum
1 x 400 g roll puff pastry
4 hardboiled eggs, sliced
salt and pepper
2 cups leftover chicken or meat, sliced into strips
1 egg, beaten

Vegetable cake

Preheat the oven to 180 °C and butter a small loaf tin or terrine dish. Beat the eggs in a large bowl. Add the semolina, cheese, origanum, salt and pepper. Dice the cooked vegetables, add to the egg mixture and mix well. Pour into the tin or dish and bake in a bain-marie for 40 minutes or until it comes away from the sides. Serve with tomato sauce.

Tip: I use a large loaf tin as a bain-marie and put a small loaf tin inside.

2 eggs
1 tbs fine semolina
2 tbs grated Cheddar cheese
a pinch of dried origanum
salt and pepper
1 cup cooked broccoli florets
1 cup cooked green beans

DeKock Meneer

'A sweet, dear old French lady gave DeKock this tip for a snack to make any time – croque monsieur. He says it helps his hangover, together with his very own regmaker.'

Butter 2 slices of crustless white bread. Make a sandwich with a few thin slices of strong Cheddar cheese and a slice of ham. Heat a little butter in a pan with a drop of oil, and brown the sandwich on both sides. Sometimes he dips the sandwich in beaten egg and then fries it until golden. Season well.

My Saffron Secret

'When I was Ambassadress to Bapetikosweti I roamed the world to promote business interest for our homeland. One of my most memorable visits was to Valencia in Spain. When I left, King Juan Carlos gave me a present of 30 saffron bulbs and said: "You'll never have to buy this expensive spice ever again." (Thank goodness for my diplomatic bag – not for the first time used to smuggle precious culinary gifts.) He was right. I planted the bulbs in a dry part of my garden and waited for the first autumn rains. What magic, seeing the green spikes push up through the ground, to be followed by this exquisite lilac-purple crocus. I collect the blooms once they've opened and pick out the red stigmas. After drying, I preserve them in an airtight jar and keep in a dark cupboard. The lilac petals are edible too and I love scattering them over a salad. I use this spice mainly in fish and rice dishes, but you can also flavour cakes and cookies with it.'

Saffron potatoes

Put the potatoes in a pot with just enough water to cover. Bring to the boil, add the saffron and salt. Cook for about 20 minutes until tender. If there is a lot of liquid left, pour into a small pot and boil to reduce to about 5 tbs. Mash the potatoes with the saffron liquid, cream and olive oil. Season to taste. Serve warm with grilled or baked fish (p. 27).

750 g floury potatoes,
   peeled and diced
¼ tsp saffron threads
a good pinch of salt
2 tbs fresh cream
1 tbs olive oil
salt and pepper

Saffron fish patties

Preheat the oven to 200 °C and grease a baking tray. Roll out the pastry and cut into six circles, 15 cm in diameter. Soak the saffron in the boiling water for 5 minutes. Sauté the leeks in a little oil until soft. In a bowl, mix the fish, leeks, breadcrumbs, salt and pepper. Stir the saffron into the melted butter and add this to the fish mixture. Spoon the mixture onto one side of the pastry, fold over the other side and pinch to seal. Use a fork to crimp the edges. Transfer to the baking tray, brush with the beaten egg and bake for 30 minutes. Serve hot or cold for a delicious snack or starter.

1 x 400 g roll puff pastry
¼ tsp saffron threads
2 tsp boiling water
1 cup thinly sliced leeks
oil
400 g cooked white fish,
   flaked
3 tbs fresh white
   breadcrumbs
salt and pepper
2 tbs melted butter
1 egg, beaten

Saffron rice

Sauté 1 small chopped onion in a little oil in a pot. Add ¼ tsp saffron threads and 1 cup rice. Add 2½ cups stock or water and bring to the boil. Reduce the heat and simmer until cooked. Cover the pot with a clean tea towel for 10 minutes to allow the grains to separate.

Jogo says:

Tummy ache: Saffron is a mild purge. Halve 2 oranges and sprinkle with saffron. Bake at 180 °C for 20 minutes. Steep the oranges overnight in 1 litre dry white wine. Strain and bottle in a sterilised jar. Drink a glass each morning for 3 days, or until cured.

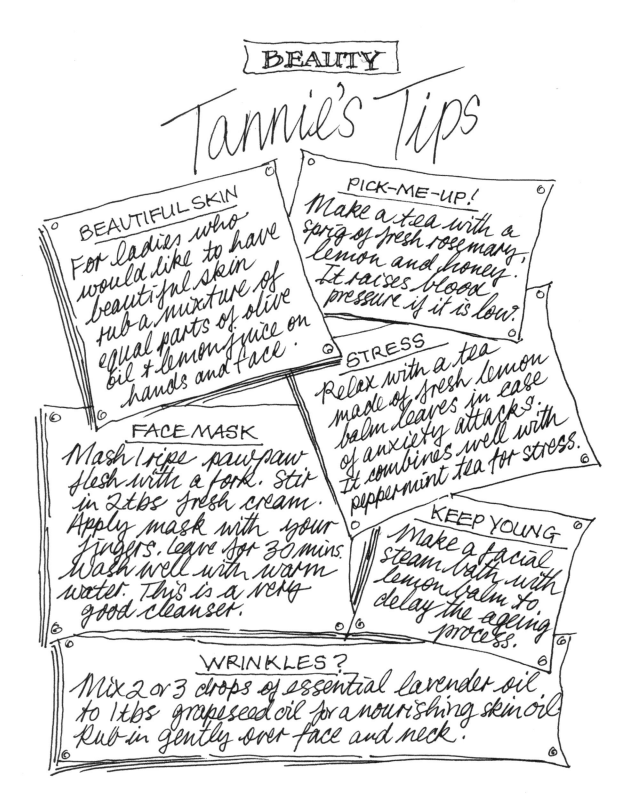

BEAUTY

Tannie's Tips

BEAUTIFUL SKIN
For ladies who would like to have beautiful skin rub a mixture of equal parts of olive oil + lemon juice on hands and face.

PICK-ME-UP!
Make a tea with a sprig of fresh rosemary, lemon and honey. It raises blood pressure if it is low.

FACE MASK
Mash 1 ripe pawpaw flesh with a fork. Stir in 2 tbs fresh cream. Apply mask with your fingers. Leave for 30 mins. Wash well with warm water. This is a very good cleanser.

STRESS
Relax with a tea made of fresh lemon balm leaves in case of anxiety attacks. It combines well with peppermint tea for stress.

KEEP YOUNG
Make a facial steam bath with lemon balm to delay the ageing process.

WRINKLES?
Mix 2 or 3 drops of essential lavender oil to 1 tbs grapeseed oil for a nourishing skin oil. Rub in gently over face and neck.

Salmagundi

'Even though I passionately love cooking and entertaining, every now and then I need a break. The family know this and enjoy bringing Sunday lunch. They love to visit Gogo! Ouma Ossewania usually makes her souttert and her dear friend, Ma Galloway's stone cream dessert. She sometimes brings her along for an outing. My daughter, Billie-Jeanne, brings her famous salmagundi platter. Her husband never goes anywhere without his isiskwamba (a little like me with my bobotie) and, of course, no lunch is complete without DeKock's raspberry tart. Mof de Bruyn is always experimenting – and all the kids go bananas as they love this mish-mash matza pudding of a lunch, contributing by creating their own desserts – this is their idea!'

Raspberries
Nutella chocolate spread
Shortbread

Billie-Jeanne's platter

'She just loves making elaborate salad platters. Her speciality is bringing different arrangements every time. This is an example of one of her imaginative arrays.'

Cover a large platter with salad leaves. Arrange roasted red pepper strips down the side of the platter. Border them with a row of cooked green beans, then a row of sliced hardboiled eggs. Continue layering the platter with rows of red cherry tomatoes, chickpeas, sliced onions, strips of stir-fried chicken breasts, cucumber rounds, chunks of feta, black olives, mushrooms, pickles and sliced salami. Decorate with fresh basil or rocket. And don't forget biltong, droëwors, baby potatoes, carrot sticks, quail eggs, anchovies ... in fact, you can use anything you fancy, contrasting the colours to make a show. Serve with a dip or two.

Dips & sauces

Herb dip
Mix 1 tbs chopped chives, 1 tbs chopped fresh mint, 3 tbs cream cheese and 1 cup buttermilk. Sprinkle with paprika.

Chilli dip
Mix 3 tbs cream cheese, 1 cup buttermilk, ½ tbs lemon juice, ¼ cup tomato paste and a few drops of Tabasco sauce to taste.

Ricotta sauce
This is good with crudités, tomatoes and boiled eggs. Mix ½ cup ricotta, ½ cup plain yoghurt, 2 tsp lemon juice, 2 tbs grated Parmesan and 1 tbs chopped fresh parsley. Season with coarsely ground black pepper.

Mustard sauce
Mix 1 tsp Dijon mustard, 1 tbs sour cream and ½ cup plain yoghurt. Season to taste.

Isiskwamba

Rinse and chop 4 cups spinach herbs and place in a big pot with 3 cups water. Bring to the boil. Add 3 cups mealie meal in a steady stream and stir. Lower the heat and simmer for about 20 minutes until the mealie meal is cooked. Stir with a fork for a crumbly texture.

Ma G's stone cream

Dissolve 2 tbs gelatine in 1 cup cold water in a large bowl and set aside for 10 minutes. Add 1½ cups boiling water, stir and leave to cool. Stir in 1 x 385 g can condensed milk, 120 ml sherry and 1 tsp vanilla essence. Pour into a mould and allow to cool before refrigerating until set.

Variation: For chocolate stone cream, add 2 tbs cocoa powder instead of vanilla essence. Dissolve the cocoa in a little hot water before adding with the condensed milk and sherry.

Raspberry tart

Butter a tart dish. Press 1 x 400 g roll shortcrust pastry into the dish and prick with a fork. Blind bake for 20 minutes and set aside to cool. Mix 300 g mascarpone cheese with 50 g castor sugar, ½ cup Bulgarian yoghurt and 1 tsp vanilla essence. Spoon onto the pastry base and decorate with 250 g raspberries. Refrigerate for 15 minutes before serving.

'The kids tell me whenever they eat spinach at home, their teeth go 'furry', but not with Gogo. "Why is that?" they ask. Because Gogo adds butter or cream to spinach dishes, that's why! First cook the washed spinach leaves in a pot or deep pan in very little water. Cover and steam for 3–4 minutes. Squeeze dry, then toss in butter or cream, or use it to stuff cannelloni, or in omelettes, etc.'

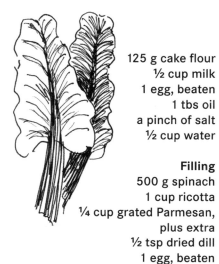

Spinach crêpe cannelloni

125 g cake flour
½ cup milk
1 egg, beaten
1 tbs oil
a pinch of salt
½ cup water

Filling
500 g spinach
1 cup ricotta
¼ cup grated Parmesan,
plus extra
½ tsp dried dill
1 egg, beaten
salt and pepper
1 cup pouring cream

Sift the flour into a bowl and make a well in the centre. Gradually add the milk, mixing slowly to incorporate. Mix in the beaten egg, oil and salt. Gradually add the water, mixing all the time to get a very smooth, liquid batter. Cover and leave to stand for 1 hour. Lightly oil a crêpe pan and spoon in 2 tbs batter. Swirl the pan so that the batter spreads out thinly and evenly. Cook over moderate heat for 1 minute, then flip and cook for a further minute. Stack the crêpes on a plate between sheets of greaseproof paper as you cook. You should get about 10 crêpes, 18 cm in diameter.

Preheat the oven to 190 °C and butter an ovenproof dish. To make the filling, cook and drain the spinach and put in a bowl. Add the ricotta, Parmesan, dill, egg, salt and pepper. Mix well. Put a line of filling on one end of a crêpe. Roll up carefully and place in the greased dish. Continue with the remaining crêpes, placing them in the dish in a single layer. Cover with the cream and sprinkle with extra Parmesan. Bake for about 15 minutes until bubbling.

Coronation chicken

½ cooked chicken
6 baby potatoes, boiled
and diced
1 cucumber, peeled and diced
4 spring onions, chopped
1 tbs chopped chives
mixed salad leaves
paprika

Dressing
½ cup plain yoghurt
1 tbs mayonnaise
2 tbs chutney
1 tbs mild curry powder
1 tsp tomato sauce
salt and pepper

'Ouma just loves making this dish – she hates wasting, so this is a perfect way of using leftover chicken – it takes her back to the 1950s! I've come up with a lighter version, using yoghurt instead of cream.'

To make the dressing, combine all the ingredients and season well. Take the chicken meat off the bone and cut into small chunks. Toss the chicken, potatoes, cucumber, spring onions and chives in the dressing. Arrange the salad leaves on a serving platter, spoon over the chicken mixture and sprinkle with paprika. Fit for a queen!

Easy macaroni cheese

Cook the macaroni al dente according to the packet instructions. Drain and set aside. Preheat the oven to 230 °C and butter an ovenproof dish well. Heat the milk and cream in a saucepan to a simmer, and then pour into a bowl. Season with nutmeg, salt and pepper. Add the macaroni and half of the grated cheese. Mix well. Pour into the greased dish and scatter over the remaining cheese. Bake for 20 minutes until golden brown. This is a very simple, quick and inexpensive dish.

Variations: Add bite-size pieces of cooked fish or chicken.

500 g macaroni
300 ml milk
1 cup pouring cream
a good pinch of ground
 nutmeg
salt and pepper
200 g Cheddar or Emmental
 cheese, grated

Cheese thyme tart

Heat the cream in a saucepan with the dried thyme. Remove from the heat and let it infuse for 30 minutes. Mix in the cottage cheese and eggs, and season to taste. Preheat the oven to 180 °C and butter a tart dish. Roll out the pastry and press into the dish. Pour over the cheese mixture. Slice the goat's cheese rolls and arrange the circles on top of the tart. Sprinkle over a pinch or two of thyme leaves. Bake for 40 minutes. Serve warm or at room temperature with a green salad topped with walnuts and a dressing of ½ tbs walnut oil, ½ tbs sunflower oil, salt, pepper and a dash of wine vinegar.

3 tbs pouring cream
1 tsp dried thyme
2 x 250 g tubs smooth
 cottage cheese
4 eggs, beaten
salt and pepper
1 x 400 g roll shortcrust
 pastry
2 x 100 g rolls goat's milk
 cheese
fresh thyme leaves

Gogo's goulash soup

Sauté the onion in the oil in a heavy-bottomed pot until translucent. Sprinkle over the paprika and stir over low heat. Add the meat and brown on all sides. Add 1 cup of the water, stir, cover and simmer for 1 hour. Add the potatoes, tomatoes, red pepper, garlic, chilli, salt, pepper and the remaining water. Simmer gently for 1 hour until the meat is very soft. Cook longer if necessary.

Variation: To make a goulash stew, add only 1 cup water with the potatoes, etc. and stir in 1 cup sour cream at the end.

1 large onion, chopped
2 tbs oil
1 tbs paprika
600 g stewing beef, cubed
5 cups water
750 g potatoes, peeled and cubed
2 tomatoes, peeled and chopped
1 red pepper, diced
2 cloves garlic, chopped
a pinch of chilli powder
salt and pepper

Spiced roast chicken

Preheat the oven to 200 °C. Place the chicken pieces on a baking tray. Combine the soy sauce, olive oil, chilli, cinnamon and lemon juice and ladle over the chicken. Put the pearl onions and whole unpeeled garlic cloves in between the chicken thighs. Cook for 35 minutes, or until the chicken is tender and cooked through.

Variation: Top the chicken with a mixture of soy sauce and honey. Tuck 4 sticks cinnamon and 4 star anise in between and sprinkle with 4 crushed cardamom pods, ground cumin and turmeric. When roasting chicken like this, you can place sweet potato or potato wedges, cubed butternut, fennel bulbs or red pepper chunks around the chicken – it's a very quick and easy way to cook for a small dinner party.

4 chicken quarters (thighs and drumsticks)
2 tbs soy sauce
2 tbs olive oil
a pinch of chilli powder
a pinch of ground cinnamon
1 tbs lemon juice
12 pearl onions
16 cloves garlic

Tongue in apricot sauce

Boil the tongue in a pot of water with the bay leaves, carrot and onion. Cook until tender and leave to cool. Preheat the oven to 180 °C. In the meantime, make the apricot sauce. If using dried apricots, soak them in water first. Halve and depip fresh apricots and put them in a saucepan with the water. Add the sugar, sultanas, vinegar, mustard and salt. Bring to the boil, and then reduce the heat and simmer, stirring frequently, until the sauce thickens. Peel the tongue and slice it finely. Spoon the apricot sauce into an ovenproof dish, spreading it out to cover the bottom, then alternate layers of tongue and sauce, ending with sauce. Heat through in the oven for 10–15 minutes. Serve with boiled potatoes and a green salad.

1 pickled beef tongue
2 bay leaves
1 large carrot, peeled and chopped
1 medium onion, chopped
12 fresh or dried apricots
1 cup water
½ cup brown sugar
a handful of sultanas
¼ cup white wine vinegar
1 tsp hot mustard
½ tsp salt

Veldkos

'When we were young, we were very poor. Ouma Ossewania would go into the veld and other people's gardens and gather a plant most people regarded as a weed – purslane. "Keep your eyes open," she'd say, "dis veldkos!" Purslane in Malawi translates as "buttocks-of-the-wife-of-a-chief" according to Dr Herklots. The plant has rounded fleshy leaves! Ouma cooked purslane like spinach with butter and cream (a bonus when she worked on the dairy farm) and sprinkled the leaves over soups and salads. Purslane tastes like fresh cucumber, yet slightly nutty, and is rich in magnesium. Try it, it's free! At the same time she collected suring (edible sorrel), which she used instead of lemon in her tasty stews, and she always kept an eye open for dandelion and prickly pears.'

Dandelion & bacon salad

Pick young dandelion leaves close to the centre of the plant. The dark green leaves are bitter, but to counteract this, soak the cut leaves in cold water overnight. Blend the garlic and vinaigrette in the bottom of a salad bowl. Wash the dandelion leaves, add them to the bowl and toss well. Make croutons by frying the bread cubes in sunflower oil until crisp and golden. Drain on paper towel. Fry the bacon until crisp and toss over the leaves along with the croutons. Add the vinegar to the pan in which you cooked the bacon and swirl to mix with the bacon fat. Pour this over the salad and serve immediately.

Variation: Add quartered hardboiled or poached eggs.

4 handfuls young dandelion
  leaves
1 clove garlic, crushed
3 tbs vinaigrette (p. 111)
3 slices stale bread, cubed
sunflower oil
smoked streaky bacon,
  diced
a dash of vinegar

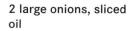

Purslane bredie

Slowly sauté the onions in oil in a heavy-bottomed pot until translucent. Add the lamb, chilli and garlic. Cover and simmer slowly for 45 minutes, adding a little water or stock now and then to keep moist. Now add the purslane, suring stalks or lemon juice and sugar. Add the potatoes and cook for a further 20 minutes until soft. Adjust the seasoning with salt, pepper and lemon juice. Decorate with fresh purslane leaves and serve with plain white rice and a sambal of chopped tomato, onion and cucumber.

2 large onions, sliced
oil
1 kg lamb shoulder, cut into
  chunks
1 dried red chilli, crushed
2 cloves garlic
2 cups chopped purslane,
  washed and thick stems
  discarded
3–4 yellow suring stalks,
  chopped, or juice of
  ½ lemon
a good pinch of sugar
2 medium potatoes, peeled
  and cut into chunks
salt, pepper and lemon juice

Prickly pear salad

Peel & slice pears. Arrange on a plate. Top with ricotta or cottage cheese.

Dribble with honey!

Ouma Says:

Bitter dandelion leaves are rich in vitamins and iron, good for rheumatism, a blood cleanser and a diuretic. The white sap can be used to treat warts. Apply regularly.

109

West Coast, my Love

'Ja-nee, Oom Kallie – he gave Pik Botha a run for his money in his youth ... ek sê maar niks ... I keep a photo of him to remind me of summer holidays. Oom Kallie is keen on predicting weather here on the West Coast. If the dried blaasoppie hanging from a nail in the ceiling of his stoep in Paternoster points northwest, he predicts rain; if it's to the southwest, the wind will blow. He has been fishing in this region for decades and still knows where to find crayfish, the best mussel rocks and where and when to go fishing for galjoen. He is a great believer in seaweed and has been digging it into his vegetable garden for years to enrich the soil, thus producing the most delicious potatoes. He makes his own seaweed jelly and pickles and cooks fish, mussels and perlemoen in hollow kelp stems.'

Fish cooked in kelp

Enjoy a walk on the beach and bring home 4 large bulbs of fresh kelp, 40 cm long. Cut kingklip or snoek fillets into chunks to fit the hollow bulbs. Fill the bulbs with pieces of fish and plug the holes with wet newspaper. Braai over very hot coals (or even flames) for 25 minutes or so, turning once or twice. Unplug and gently slide out the steamed fish. Experiment! I learnt to wrap food in vine leaves from my friend Beulah in De Doorns, so why not wrap fish in seaweed, I thought. Wrap whole fish (such as kabeljou) in large, fresh kelp leaves and braai as above. Serve with potatoes cooked in foil on the fire, butter, sea salt and black pepper.

Snoek

Gadidja gave me her ouma's tip on how to cook snoek. As the flesh is rich and oily, soak the vlekked snoek in salted, lukewarm water for 2 hours before cooking, so that the oil floats to the surface. Dry well with paper towel. Fry in medium-hot oil until golden brown, turning once. Season with sea salt, black pepper and a squeeze of lemon juice.

Snoek salad

Boil potatoes in their skins. Cool, peel and cut into small chunks. Flake smoked, grilled or fried snoek, taking care to remove all the bones. Combine with the potatoes, chopped spring onions and chopped hardboiled eggs in a salad bowl.

Vinaigrette: Make a vinaigrette dressing by mixing together 1 tsp Dijon mustard, a good pinch of salt, 2 tbs oil and ½ tsp red wine vinegar. Pour into the salad and toss gently.

Oom Kallie says:

Soak in a hot bath with a few pieces of fresh kelp to relieve arthritis and rheumatism.

Seafood sauce

½ cup mayonnaise
½ cup crème fraîche
3 tbs tomato sauce
1 tsp Dijon mustard
a few drops of Tabasco sauce
a few drops of Worcestershire sauce

Mix and season with salt and pepper.

Avocado Ritz Crayfish cocktail

'Crayfish is at its most delicious braaied fresh on the beach, but I love serving this retro cocktail classic as an hors d'oeuvre to remind me of entertaining the hoi polloi with Hasie in the fifties.'

Cook crayfish in a pot half-filled with boiling water. Simmer for 15 minutes, depending on size. Crayfish will be more steamed than boiled. Take care not to overcook. Remove the flesh from the tails and legs and toss in seafood sauce. Halve and depip avocados and spoon the crayfish mixture into the hollows. Sprinkle with paprika and chopped fresh parsley.

Harders

The harder fishing season opens in October. Bokkoms are harders salted with coarse salt and dried in the breeze. Buy bokkoms already cleaned and cut into strips. They are an acquired taste – very salty and fishy, a kind of fish biltong. It's very original to serve harders in strips with chilled white wine as an apéritif. I sometimes snip them into pieces and scatter them over snoek salad (p. 111).

On the braai

Oom Kallie collects wild fennel in the veld outside Vredenburg. He dries the stems and ties them into neat little bundles, which he puts on top of the coals to flavour braaied fish.

One of the best ways to cook fresh harders is on the braai. Baste the fish with oil and sea salt and braai for about 3 minutes each side until the skin blisters. Serve with lemon wedges and eat with your fingers.

Spicy harders

Make a paste by mixing together 1 tsp chilli powder, 1 tsp turmeric, 1 tsp masala, 1 small grated onion, crushed garlic, lemon juice and olive oil. Spread over the fish, inside and out, and grill or braai over medium heat, turning once – about 3 minutes each side.

Fennel oil

Put a few dried fennel fronds and dried fennel sticks into a bottle with olive oil. Keep in a dark cupboard for 2 weeks. Drizzle over fish.

'How to describe the ozone-kelp-salty smell of the Atlantic air, mingled with wood smoke from the braai, the aroma of boerewors, lamb chops or freshly caught fish and the scent of fynbos ...? I often take my grandchildren to the beach. One day one of them brought home a crab in a bucket of sea water and left it outside in the sun. Three days later, we found a dried crab in a layer of salt. Eureka! Who would have thought that it is so easy to make salt.'

Make your own salt

Here is my easy recipe for this magical, essential ingredient which we use to flavour and preserve, and as a medicine and household cleaner. Boil 4 litres fresh, clean sea water until 80 per cent has evaporated. Pour into a flat pan or dish and leave out in the hot sun. Scoop off the thin layer on top for *fleur de sel* flakes and keep the dried bottom layer for top-quality rock salt.

Flavoured salt

Mix sea salt with spices such as ground dried red chillies, cumin and coriander, or herbs such as crushed fennel seeds (delicious over fish) and rosemary (to sprinkle over potatoes). Experiment! Try drying seaweed – crush and add to sea salt or add some turmeric when boiling the sea water for a beautiful sunshine colour.

Evita's Darling potatoes

Preheat the oven to 180 °C. Slice potatoes without cutting them all the way through and place a bay leaf in each slit. Place the potatoes on a bed of rock salt in an ovenproof dish. Drizzle with olive oil and season with sea salt and black pepper. Bake for 45 minutes. You can also use chopped rosemary, crushed garlic or bacon rashers.

BAY LEAF
POTATO
ROCKSALT

Tannie Says:

For a sore throat, gargle with salt water. Mix crushed rock salt and olive oil for a face or hand scrub.

Let's go Birdwatching!

'When I need a break from all my responsibilities, family, government business, charities, etc. I pack a picnic, get into my car and drive up to the West Coast National Park or to Velddrif, to go birdwatching. I still haven't spotted the little blue heron that lives in front of the hotel, but you never know ... During summer months, the Langebaan Lagoon is home to a greater diversity of species of waders (birds that feed between the low- and high-water mark) than almost anywhere else on the planet. Most of these birds will have flown 14 000 km from their breeding grounds in the Russian Tundra.'

Birdwatching snack
Mix almonds, sunflower seeds, pumpkin seeds, black currants or golden sultanas and/or dried cranberries and put into small sandwich bags to nibble while waiting for the tide to go out.

Cooking for the birds

'I have 35 different species of bird in my garden in Darling. If you want to encourage birds to your garden, the first thing to do is to plant indigenous trees and shrubs, supplying a natural source of food for seed, nectar and insect eaters throughout the year. Almost more important than food is a supply of fresh, clean water. Birds need to bath in order to keep their feathers in tip-top shape. Put bells around your cats' necks – and remind neighbours to do the same.'

Bird food

Take a big pine cone and fill the cavities with peanut butter. Press sunflower seeds or any other bird seed into the peanut butter. Hang it from a shady branch at least one metre from the ground.

Fig & nut cake

120 g hazelnuts, toasted, 90 g almonds, toasted, 120 g dried figs, 3 eggs, ½ cup sugar, 120 g mixed citrus peel, 90 g dark chocolate, grated, 1¼ cups self-raising flour, sifted

Preheat the oven to 190 °C and butter a loaf tin. Roughly chop the nuts and figs. Whisk the eggs and sugar in a bowl until white and fluffy. Add the nuts, figs, peel and chocolate and stir gently until well combined. Carefully fold in the flour. Spoon the mixture into the tin and bake for 1 hour until golden brown. A skewer inserted into the centre should come out clean. Leave to cool in the tin before turning out onto a wire rack to cool completely. Cut the cake when cold and pack into your picnic basket.

Lard balls

Melt lard in a pan over low heat. Once melted, add dried, unsweetened fruit, seeds, bacon or cheese rind and stir well. Half-fill small empty yoghurt tubs with the mixture and leave to cool. Remove from the tubs and place on your bird table or hang from a tree.

Pasta carbonara

'Tide waits for no man! If we rush out to the bird hide before breakfast, with only coffee and rusks to keep the wolf from the door, we have our bacon and eggs with pasta, for lunch.'

4 rashers rindless bacon or pancetta, 1 tbs butter, ½ cup fresh cream, a pinch of paprika, 1 egg, 1 egg yolk, 60 g Parmesan, grated, 300 g fettuccine or tagliatelle, salt and black pepper

Cut the bacon or pancetta into strips and cook in the butter over low heat in a heavy-bottomed frying pan until crisp. Add the cream and paprika. Combine the egg, egg yolk and half of the Parmesan in a bowl. Cook the pasta according to the packet instructions, drain and pour into a serving bowl. Pour over the bacon mixture and toss. Add the egg mixture and mix well. Season and sprinkle over the remaining cheese.

Fynbos Botany

'Ma Joey is a fountain of knowledge. There she lives in Hopefield, in a house surrounded by prickly pears, thus avoiding the expense of a modern security system. She learnt all about the veld and fynbos from her oupa, who claimed to be a descendant of Henry Lichtenstein, but maybe it is just a case of too much Stein!

'The medicinal properties of plants are found in the volatile or essential oils in their leaves, flowers, fruit, stems and roots, which makes certain plants the basis of the medicine chest. Infusions from fresh or dried plant material aid digestion, relieve respiratory problems, make soothing inhalations and provide mildly antiseptic skin lotions or gargles. Here are some well-known plants and their uses. Remember – don't go into the veld to collect and experiment without an old hand to teach you. Traditional healers normally collect plants and prescribe remedies themselves.

'We must protect Cape flora – our precious fynbos, which occurs nowhere else on the planet!'

Buchu

Decoctions, infusions and tinctures are made from fresh or dried leaves and twigs. Good as a treatment for mild cystitis, improves digestion, and stimulates kidney and liver function. Fresh leaves can be chewed to relieve stomach problems. And buchu brandy is a cure for all!

Kukumakranka

The ripe, fleshy fruits are gathered in early winter and can be eaten fresh. Highly aromatic, they have a very sweet, fruity odour and are used to make perfume. Kukumakranka brandy is one of the early Cape remedies for colic and indigestion.

Wild rosemary

Also known as the Cape snow bush, the leaves are mildly spicy and go well with meat dishes. Cape chamomile is the essential oil of this plant and is used in perfume. Good as a shampoo to stimulate hair growth and to cure sores on the scalp. Mix 1 tbs fresh leaves to 1 cup boiling water for a general health tonic. Drink ½ cup twice a day.

Sour figs

There are several types of this creeping plant found mainly along the beach dunes and in sandy spots. Some have yellow flowers, others red. Juice from the leaves is used to treat various skin conditions, open wounds and bluebottle stings, and as a gargle for sore throats and mouth infections. The fruit is used to make jam and can be eaten fresh too.

Cancer bush

A couple of handfuls of fresh or dried leaves and young stems boiled for 30 minutes and taken after meals will boost the immune system. Used in the treatment of HIV/AIDS, kidney disease, diabetes mellitus type 2, fever, gout, rheumatism, arthritis, urinary tract infection and cystitis. It is well worth studying this bush.

Suikerbossie protea

To make bossie stroop, shake the sugar nectar from the Suikerbossie protea into a bowl. Add water and boil it down to make a syrup for cough relief.

Renosterbossie

A tea is prepared from fresh or dried flowers and leaves as a treatment for flu, indigestion, lack of appetite and stomach ulcers.

'It seems to me that nowadays many people have lost their connection with nature. When we were young, Ouma Ossewania took us for long walks in the veld, collecting veldkos along the way – dandelions, purslane, veldkool (wild cabbage), fennel and nettle – with which she made a healthy soup. We chewed yellow-flowered suring (edible sorrel), which tasted like sherbet to us. Now and then, when she had toothache, she went on the hunt for kraalbossie. She chewed the leaves and soft twigs for pain relief.

The Cape floral kingdom is an incredibly rich, biodiverse region (there are 2 200 species on and around Table Mountain – more than in the entire United Kingdom). All those lovely names – kukumakranka, kambro, baroe and bietou – are thanks to the Khoisan who, like the San, had a beautifully close connection to nature. We must try to find it again to enrich our busy lives. Slow down, stop, smell and listen: listen to the sound of the wind through the restios, inhale the smell of the fynbos, taste the salty sea breeze and gaze in wonder at this enormous gift that is nature. Unfortunately, certain fynbos species have been harvested to extinction. Never pick any indigenous plants without a permit from the Department of Environmental Affairs. More than 1 000 species are endangered. Their conservation should be a priority. If not, our grandchildren will not experience the wonderful diversity of this unique floral kingdom.'

Plakkie–Dog's ear

Fresh leaves are not collected in the dry season, but rather after good rains when they can be eaten as a snack. Drops of warmed leaf juice can be used to soothe tooth- and earache. Fresh leaf juice, swallowed once a day, soothes a sore throat.

Yellow sage

The fresh leaves have a smell of lemon-pepper and can be used in cooking. Fresh or dried leaves and twigs are boiled to make a tea that relieves asthma.

Bitter aloe

Yellow juice collected from the leaves is used for skin treatments, conjunctivitis, herpes and shingles. It is an antiseptic and can be used to cleanse open wounds.

Cape geranium

Infusions are used to treat bladder infections, venereal diseases and menstruation-related complaints.

Wild wormwood

The flowers, young stems, and fresh or dried leaves are used to make medicinal tisanes for sore throats, asthma, colds, fever, flu, malaria, headaches and colic. It can also be used in a steam bath for inhalation.

Restios for thatching

The beautiful reed grasses ('restios'), such as broom reed, Albertinia reed and Cape thatching reed, are used as thatching. These robust reeds, 1–2 metres long, are cut at the end of the growing season and used as roofing material that can last 70 years.

Cooking for Two

'When Billie-Jeanne, DeKock and Izan finally left home
to fend for themselves, Hasie and I breathed a sigh of
relief – romantic dinners for two again that remind us
of our honeymoon and life as newlyweds. Just the two
of us sitting opposite each other at the dining table.
I even changed my shopping habits. When the kids
were there, the fridge and pantry were stockpiled with
everything under the sun. I regularly bulk-shopped
to feed so many mouths, not only the kids, but their
friends as well. Now shopping is a pleasure, as I can
use fresh, seasonal ingredients. But don't feel that
cooking for two always means what it says. Treat
yourself to a romantic feast, just you – and you. You
can dress for the occasion, or not, because remember,
being on your own always means you will look your
best – for you.'

Beef & ginger stir-fry

Sprinkle the steak slices with a little oil and soy sauce. Heat the oil in a wok and stir-fry the ginger and steak over high heat for 2 minutes. Stir in the soy sauce, sugar, sherry and cornflour mixture and stir-fry for 1 minute. Add the spring onions and stir a few more times. Serve hot with plain rice.

250 g rump steak, finely sliced
2 tbs oil
3 cm piece fresh ginger, grated
2 tbs soy sauce
1 tsp sugar
2 tbs dry sherry
1 tsp cornflour dissolved in 1 tsp water
3 spring onions, chopped

Pot-roasted quail

'Nothing is more suited to roasting two plump quails than my small, oval copper pot. It has sentimental value, as it was a gift from Yves St Laurent when we hit it off in Paris after a fashion show.'

Brown the quails in the duck fat or oil over low heat and cook for 10 minutes. Cut the carrots into thick sticks about 3 cm long and add to the pot, along with the onion and rosemary. Season, cover and continue cooking for another 15 minutes or so, stirring and turning the quails gently. Halve the garlic cloves without removing the skins and add to the pot. Cover and cook for a further 5 minutes, or until done. I like to serve straight from my beautiful pot, otherwise transfer to a serving platter. This is delicious with saffron rice (p. 99) or roast potatoes.

2 plump quails
2 tbs duck fat or oil
2 carrots, peeled
1 medium onion, chopped
2 sprigs rosemary
salt and pepper
8 large cloves garlic

Pasta mortadella

'Hasie adores mortadella! This pasta dish is quick and easy and I often make it to please him after a long day out.'

Combine the butter and cream in a saucepan over low heat, stirring until the butter has melted. Add the Parmesan and mortadella strips, and season. Cook the penne according to the packet instructions, drain and pour over the sauce. Toss well. Grate over a little nutmeg and serve immediately with extra Parmesan at the table.

90 g butter
2/3 cup fresh cream
90 g Parmesan, grated, plus extra
4 slices mortadella, cut into strips
salt and pepper
300 g penne pasta
freshly grated nutmeg

The Charlize Theron Africa Outreach Project

'Charlize has not only adopted a little boy called Jackson, she has adopted the children of South Africa.'

The Charlize Theron Africa Outreach Project helps keep African youth safe from HIV/AIDS by supporting and collaborating with community-based organisations that address the key drivers of the disease.

charlize theron
AFRICA OUTREACH PROJECT

For more information visit www.charlizeafricaoutreach.org
Facebook: www.facebook.com/charlizeafricaoutreachproject
Twitter: @CharlizeAfrica

122

The Darling Trust

' Authors' royalties from *Evita's Kossie Sikelela* and this new book go to The Darling Trust, so let me tell you more about what you are helping.

The Darling Trust was established in August 2003 by Evita se Perron to assist the previously disadvantaged communities of our town. We aim to empower people to help themselves mainly through our focus on education, health and skills development. Nothing happens in ten minutes, maar aanhouer wen. After nearly ten years, The Darling Trust is celebrating so many success stories among our children, their parents and the whole community of Darling, irrespective of colour or creed.

We want to keep ourselves healthy and strong through education and care. We encourage each other to develop talents and skills. We assist one another to cope with the challenges of today: HIV/AIDS, TB, poverty, survival and fear. And already other small communities are looking at our blueprint and taking inspiration from The Darling Trust.

You have helped us all by buying this book. You can always buy three more and send them to your children and grandchildren in Australia, the USA, Canada, the UK and Europe. Just write in the front: "Kom huis toe. Tannie Evita se kos is op die tafel!"

We would also welcome your contributions to assist us in making dreams come true. '

PO Box 175, Darling, 7345, South Africa

Darling Station, Arcadia Street, Darling, 7345, South Africa

Telephone + 27 (0)22 492 3384

Fax +27 (0)86 691 9543

info@thedarlingtrust.org

Banking details
Bank: Standard Bank, Branch: Darling, Branch code: 05-01-11
Swift code: SBZAZAJJ
Account name: The Darling Trust
Account no.: 08-326-482-5

Registration details
Registered in terms of Section 6 (1) of the Trust Property Control Act 1988 (Act 57 of 1988)
No.: IT 2598/2003
PBO 930 187 22, 054 -755 - NPO

Please visit our website and see how you can help: www.thedarlingtrust.org.

Acknowledgements

'My granddaughter, Winnie-Jeanne Makoeloeli, is doing very well in Art at school and has prepared all the clever little collages in this book, taking my face and sticking me onto a variety of bodies! Her gogo is very grateful for her thoughtful, kind choices.

My greatest debt is to my mother, Ouma Ossewania, who taught me how to make a little go a long way. I owe so much to our Rainbow Nation, which always existed but needed Madiba and Archbishop Tutu to bring it forth! Thank you to all the people I met on my travels whose food I've tasted, who gave me life-saving tips and advice, recipes, and secrets. Their generosity knew no bounds. They inspire me to write cookbooks and I wish to acknowledge my debt of gratitude here.

Thank you to Beulah, Oom Simmie, Carole, Johannetjie, Dulcie, Ouma Elise, Oom Rudi, Oom Septie, Tannie Katie, Missi Hu, Mama Maiti, Mimi, Tannie Dot, Leyla and Nadia, Alice, Sophia, Queenie, Maggie, Rosa, Liam, Bradley, Rebecca, Pik, Mof, Ma Galloway, Hannahkins, Bennie, Oom Kallie, Gadidja, Ma Joey, Frederik, Fourie, Marius, Stefan, Uda, and Johanne and George of the famous Al Forno Restaurant, Providence, USA, and last but not least my wonderful multicultural family. Also to the !Khwa ttu San Cultural Centre for use of their publication *Gathering Fynbos, Ethnobotany of the San*.

Remember, smell the fynbos, and keep cooking and creating – there's no better recipe for hope, and the belief that everything will turn out beautifully in the end, than a loving, well-cooked dinner shared around the table.

Hamba kahle!'

Glossary

bain-marie – a double-boiler or water bath used for cooking food through evenly, e.g. terrines and egg-based dishes. A large pan filled with hot but not boiling water, in which the cooking dish rests. The whole thing is then placed in the oven

béchamel sauce – a white sauce made by cooking flour and butter over low heat and adding milk to make a smooth, lightly thickened sauce. The sauce has to be well whisked to prevent lumps forming

biltong – dried strips of beef, game or ostrich meat flavoured with coriander seeds

boerewors – beef, or beef and pork sausages flavoured with coriander

blaasoppie – pufferfish

bokkoms – a kind of fish biltong made from salted harders dried in the breeze

bon vivant – a good-tempered, jovial person who enjoys fine food and wine as well as a good, luxurious life

braai – a barbecue

caul – the lace-like fatty membrane that surrounds a pig or sheep's stomach. Used to wrap food for cooking, grilling, braising or roasting

Campari – a bitter, red alcoholic Italian apéritif often mixed with soda or fresh orange juice

caramelise – to carefully heat sugar until it turns brown and syrupy

clafoutis – a French dessert usually consisting of black cherries covered in a thick pancake batter and baked

compote – a preparation of fresh fruit, whole, or cut into chunks, then poached in a sugar syrup. Fruit can also be puréed once cooked

confit – seasoned fruit or vegetables usually cooked to a jam-like consistency, also meat or poultry cooked and preserved in its own fat

coulis – a liquid purée of cooked fruit or vegetables

court-bouillon – a French name for stock or broth

crème de cassis – a liqueur made from black currants originating in Burgundy, France

crème fraîche – a slightly sharp-tasting, thick double cream, less sour than sour cream

croque monsieur – a toasted ham and cheese sandwich

croutons – small cubes of bread that have been fried in oil or butter, and then toasted or dried in the oven

droëwors – dried beef or game sausage

Evita's Kossie Sikelela – Evita Bezuidenhout's first cookbook

fata morgana – an Italian term for a mirage seen in a narrow band above the horizon distorting the landscape or seascape

fleur de sel – the crystals that float on the surface of salty sea water, harvested by hand after evaporation. A fine, quality sea salt

Hamba kahle – Go well! in Zulu

hardekool or doringboom – hard wood or wood from thorn trees used for braaing

hors d'œuvre – an appetiser, starter or savoury tidbit

Idols – a talent show seen on TV

isiskwamba – a wild spinach herb and mealie meal combination

korrelkonfyt – grape jam

mampoer – a fruit brandy usually made from peaches, apricots or prickly pears

morogo – African wild spinach-type herbs, e.g. stinging nettle, wild mustard

mortadella – a lightly smoked Italian sausage, 15 cm in diameter, made of ground pork and beef, diced with fat and studded with pistachio nuts or green olives

Orania – a small exclusive Afrikaner 'homeland' settlement in the Northern Cape

padkos – a beloved word for picnic food for the road

piperade – sweet peppers and tomatoes cooked in olive oil, mixed with beaten eggs and lightly scrambled

purée – to mash vegetables or fruit into a creamy, thick preparation

putupap – a mealie meal porridge cooked dry then eaten crumbly or stiff with sauce or boerewors

ragoût – a thickish liquidy stew made from meat, poultry or vegetables, all cut into equal sizes

rissoles – Seasoned minced cooked meat, fish, vegetables or pulses made into patties or balls, coated in breadcrumbs or flour, then fried or deep-fried

salmagundi – an elaborate salad with many different ingredients arranged attractively on a large platter. Also applies to a dinner attended by several families or friends each bringing their own dish. A hotchpotch!

semolina – granules of coarsely ground maize or hard durum wheat

Spanish tortilla – a potato omelette cut into quarters like a tart

sumac – used in Middle Eastern cooking; a purple-red powder with an acid taste that is used instead of lemon juice

tabouleh – a Lebanese salad made with burghal (cracked wheat), tomatoes, spring onions, chopped mint and parsley, garlic, olive oil and lemon juice

tapenade – a purée made with olives, capers and anchovies pounded together with olive oil and a drop of brandy

terrine – a deep rectangular or oval dish with a tight-fitting lid used for cooking mixed meat, fish or vegetables. Usually cooked in a bain-marie. Food prepared in this way is named after the dish in which it is cooked, hence 'terrine'

Van Der Hum – a South African brandy-based liqueur made from naartjies

vinaigrette – a dressing for salads made with vinegar, oil and salt, to which mustard, herbs or garlic may be added

vlei – a shallow, seasonal pond or marsh

waterblommetjies – a water hyacinth found growing wild in vleis in the Cape

Register

Published in 2012 by Umuzi
an imprint of Random House Struik (Pty) Ltd
Company Reg No. 1966/003153/07
Wembley Square, First Floor, Solan Road, Gardens,
Cape Town 8001
PO Box 1144, Cape Town 8000, South Africa
umuzi@randomstruik.co.za
www.randomstruik.co.za

First edition, first printing 2012
9 8 7 6 5 4 3 2 1

ISBN 978-1-4152-0156-5

Original design by Linda Vicquery
Cover design and layout by mr design
Cover photograph of Evita by
Pat Bromilow-Downing
Set in Corporate
Printed and bound by Tien Wah Press, Singapore

Ook in Afrikaans, as *Evita se bossie sikelela*

Photographs by Linda Vicquery (pp. 46, 52, 72,
and backgrounds on pp. 12, 18, 21, 26, 74, 110);
Elise Barlow (p. 15); Stefan Hurter (pp. 16, 22, 80,
84, 87, 110, 112, 114, 119, 120, 128); Uda Strydom
(pp. 36, 48, 50, 69, 82, 98, 102, 111, 113, 116, and
backgrounds on pp. 16, 27, 30, 56, 112, 114); Pat
Bromilow-Downing (pp. 8, 28, 45, 76); Kelly Walsh
(pp. 38, 105); *Rooi Rose* (p. 54); Ruphin Coudyzer
(pp. 67, 85); Merwelene van der Merwe (p. 117);
and Angela Buckland (p. 122).

Paintings of Evita in the style of the masters by
Nina van der Westhuizen are: *American Gothic* by
Grant Wood, 1930 (p. 34); a woman by Maggie
Laubser (p. 58); *Whistler's Mother* by James
McNeill Whistler, 1871 (p. 60); *Gypsy Woman with
Baby* by Amedeo Modigliani, 1919 (p. 70); and
Woman with Plants by Grant Wood, 1929 (p. 108).